MISSISSIPPI COURT RECORDS,

1799 - 1835

By
J. Estelle Stewart King

JANAWAY PUBLISHING, INC.
Santa Maria, California
2006, 2018

Notice

In many older books, foxing (or discoloration) occurs and, in some instances, print lightens with wear and age. Reprinted books, such as this, often duplicate these flaws, notwithstanding efforts to reduce or eliminate them. For this book, specifically, the original edition was mimeographed and, as with most all mimeographed pages, the print is often uneven and over-inked, resulting in smears and difficult to read text. The pages of this reprint have been digitally enhanced and, where possible, the flaws eliminated in order to provide clarity of content and a pleasant reading experience.

TABLE OF CONTENTS

PREFACE

J. Estelle Stewart King was a prolific writer and compiler of genealogical material and books in the 1930s. Though many of her published works covered material in the states of Kentucky and Virginia, her focus was generally on areas where published information was cursory or scarce. This present offering is such a work.

This book, which was originally published in 1936, consists of abstracts of court and other miscellaneous records from the early Mississippi counties of Adams, Amite, Claiborne, Hinds, Warren, and Yalobusha. With the exception of Claiborne County, which produced no offspring, these counties were the parent counties, in whole or part, of what is now Copiah, Franklin, Greene, Grenada, Lincoln, Rankin and Wilkinson counties.

At the end of this work an index has been provided. Please note, however, the names of males in the marriage records and tax list are not included, since these two records are published in alphabetical order. When searching for an individual's name, the researcher should first look at the index, and then the marriage records and the tax list to determine if their subject is included in the text.

Janaway Publishing, Inc.
Santa Maria, California, 2006

DEDICATED

To The Memory

of

MY GRANDMOTHER

MARTHA COCKE STEWART

————

Whose parents were among the early
pioneers of Mississippi Territory.

————

Born October 31, 1817.
Died April 9, 1908.

NOTE

In the Wills the first date given is the date of the
instrument, the second date of probate. Few abbrevi-
ations have been used and these are obvious: Wit.-
Witness, Exr.- Executor and Executrix, Apprs.-Apprai-
sers, Admr.-Administrator.

The names of the men in the Marriage Records and Tax
List are arranged alphabetically and are not given in
the Index, but the names of the women in Marriage Records
are indexed.

ADAMS COUNTY

WILLS

1799-1801

MILLER, JOSEPH

Jan. 25, 1799. April 20, 1799.
Estate to wife (not named).
Children: William and Hannah.
Wit: Nathan Wright, Giles Andrews, Charles Marr
and John McDonald.

GRAY, RUFFIN.

Nov. 20, 1798.
Wife: Lucy Gray. Son: Ruffin. Dau: Mary Ann Gray.
Exrs: son Ruffin, Alexander Starling, Robert Cochrane,
Philip Gray.
Wit: Joseph Dove, Solomon Alston, William Conner.

BENOIST, GABRIEL

Feb. 25, 1798. July, 1799.
Planter. Wife: Elizabeth (Dunbar) Benoist. Brother:
Francois Rene Benoist. Mention is made of property
inherited from father, Pierre Benoist.
Exrs: wife, Robert Dunbar (father-in-law), William Dun-
bar, William George Fitzgerald. Wit: John Brisbane,
Charles Boardman, David Greenleaf, Jonathan Jones, David
Ferguson and Peter Walker.

OWENS, WILLIAM

Sept. 21, 1799. -----
Wife: Susannah Owens. Children: Andrew, Alexander, Nancy,
William and James, to have entire estate. Children: Martin,
Margaret, Mary and Dorcas, to have $5. each.
Exrs: wife, John Bisland, George Fitzgerald.
Wit: Robert Taylor and Eustace Humphreys.

WALTON, GEORGE.

Jan. 18, 1800. May, 1800.
All estate to son, Jack Walton and daughter-in-law.

SWAYNE, SAMUEL.

February 7, 1794. -----
Wife: Elizabeth, to have plantation, household goods
and furniture. Sons: John, James, Samuel and Daniel.
Dau: Elizabeth. Wit: John Short, Adam Cloud, Joseph
Duncan, John McChristy, Samuel Chichester, William
Taylor and Andrew Scanlon.

WITHERS, ROBERT.

April 14, 1800. ----
Wife: Dicey Withers. Legatees: Esther Turner, Eanes
(children), Hollingsworth Withers (bro.), Mary and
Sarah (sisters). Exrs: James Wade, Jesse Withers and
Robert Turner.

CALLAHAN, ELIZABETH.

February 11, 1798. ---
Formerly of Lunenburg Co., Va. Legatees: John and
David Callahan (sons), Betsy and Susannah (daus.),
Thomas Griffin and John Callahan (gr.sons).
Exrs: sons John and David. Wit: James White and John
Shepherd.

FORMAN, GENERAL DAVID.

August 30, 1796.
Of Chester Town, Maryland. To daughter Sarah Marsh For-
man, all furniture and plate. Mention is made of wife
Ann Forman. Daughters: Ann, Emma, Eliza, Malvina, Ri-
vina. Sister Margaret Forman, widow of brother Ezekiel
Forman, dec'd. Exrs: daughter Sarah Marsh Foreman and
her husband, William Gordon Foreman.
Wit: Phil Reed, William Burnett, Ben Chambers.

NICHOLSON, JAMES.

March 13, 1801. April, 1801.
Legatees: brother Henry Nicholson and nephew Henry Nic-
holson- estate to be given the seven children of brother Henry Nicholson: William, Watkins, James, Mary,
Samuel, Pamelia and Henry. Nephew Nicholson, son of Edmund Harris and wife Mary, of Bute County, North Carolina. Freedom given to 2 old slaves. "My desire is
that my poor slaves, who have always been treated tender-
ly by me, shall be used with humanity." Exrs: Hugh Davis,
Marsham Ellis, Ben Farrar. Wit: Matt McCullock, Landon
Davis and Patrick Foley.

STACLPOOL, MAURICE.

28 June, 1800. June Court, 1801.
Legatees: wife Juliana, Pierce Stackpool (bro. living
near Dublin, Ireland).
Exrs: David Ferguson, George Cochrane, Milling Wooley.
Wit: Sam Timberlake, Henry Turner, D. Lattimore.

ORR, JAMES.

June 8, 1801. 10 June, 1801.
"All effects to be put in the hands of John Beesland
and William ----(?) (probably William Dunbar).
Wit: John Beesland and William Dunbar, Jr.

DAVIDSON, JOHN B.

Of Kentucky. Probated August 6, 1801.
Legatees: Bazel Crow, Benjamin Kitchen (half-brother),
Williams Weathers. Exr: Bazel Crow.
Wit: Richard May, Samuel May.

ELLIS, RICHARD.

October 17, 1792.---------
To wife, Mary Ellis, plantation at White Cliff (1000
acres)and a large number of slaves.
Dau: Jane, to have 25 negroes; to dau. Mary, plantation;
Mary and Martha, daughters of dau. Martha, 25 negroes
each; to Mary, widow of son William Cocke Ellis, dec'd.,
to have balance of debts due me in Virginia.
Sons: John, Richard and Abraham. Exrs: sons John and
Abraham. Wit: Thomas Burling, John H. White, Sam Dav-
enport, Richard Duvall, John Ellis, Sr., John Dinsbrey.

SOREO, DOMINGO.

A native of the village of Santiago de Olivera, near
the town of Terry, in the Kingdom of Galicia, Spain.
Legatees: son Juan Soreo; natural dau. Sopina, two years
of age (by Catherine Lambert Segovia); a natural son
Lewis (by a woman named Jenny Bullin); to mulatto boy
Edward, son of a negro woman owned by Dr. Taverot,
$200. Exr: James Beauvais.

BAYS, ANDREW.

Nov. 2, 1801. Nov. 10, 1801.
Estate to bro. Elihu Hall Bays, Esq., of S.Carolina.
Exr: John Hutchin. Wit: Daniel Ryan, James Saunders.

PIPES, ALNOR.

November 21, 1802. No date of probate.
Wife: Mary, to have the entire management of the estate.
Daughters: Ann Pipes and Polly Pipes.
Exrs: William Foster and Richard Curtis.
Wit: Eustace Humphrey, John Pipes and Moses Kedey.

COLLINS, ISAAC, SR.

October 23,1802. June Court, 1803.
Wife: Frances Collins. Sons: Benjamin, Vinis, Robert and
Isaac. Daughters: Katey Douglas, Nancy Rice, Lucy Hall.
Exrs: wife, Benjamin Collins and Cato Wist.
Wit: Joseph Clermont and James Griffin.

VANSDAN, WILLIAM.

July 2, 1802. October 9, 1802.
Wife: Elisa, to have land, personalty and slaves, except
Ben, who is to be free.
Sisters: Ella, Catherine and Betsy.
Exrs: Ferdinand L. Claiborne, D. Latimer, Jonathan Kear-
sley.

CONNELLY, REDMOND.

September 14, 1802. June 9, 1803.
Legatee: Estate to dear and beloved friend, Daniel Fow-
ler, who is also named as executor.
Wit: John Cahill and Jonathan Salyar (?).

ROBERTS, JOHN.

November 15, 1802. June 14, 1803.
Wife: Mary, to have slaves, also money and slaves in-
herited from grandfather, William Duncan, all in the
possession of uncle William Roberts, of Culpepper County,
Virginia.
Godson: James Stewart, Jr., to inherit all the estate
after decease of wife.
Exrs: wife, James Stewart, Gerrard Branson, William
Lemmon.
Wit: William Bean, William Hay, Lucretia Stewart.

MOORE, MICHAEL.

March 20, 1803. June, 1803.
Legatees: 2/3 of all property to be divided between
Charles McBride and Thomas Jackson, remaining 1/3 to
daughter Polly Moore.
Exrs: Charles McBride and Thomas Jackson.
Wit: David Nesbitt, David Johnston, William Mitchell.

LAUGHERY, WILLIAM.

April 8, 1803. June 15, 1803.
"Of Ireland and now a citizen of the United States."
Legatees: to faithful friends John Nichols and Charles
McBride, both of Mississippi Territory, 400 acres in
Pennsylvania and authorized to obtain same from Alexan-
der McDowell, also farming implements; John Sweeny to
have $100.
Wit: Benjamin Stokes, Thomas Jackson, Anthony Ferncy.

WEIR, JAMES.

March 19, 1803. June 15, 1803.
"Dear Sir: In case any accident shall occur to take me
from this life, I wish you to take my things under your
care and remit whatever money belonging to me after settlement with Dr. Pendergrass, to my father. By taking this
trouble you will oblige my father and he will ever consider
himself your sincere friend."

MORGAN, WILLIAM.

June 13, 1803. August 13, 1803.
Of Frederick Town, County of Washington, State of Pennsylvania, now residing and being in Natchez, Mississippi
Territory, having brought with me divers goods and chattels, monies and personal estate. All estate to be sold and
proceeds sent to wife Elizabeth Morgan, to be divided
between her and the children. Also all property in Pennsylvania and Ohio to be administered by wife and friend
Isaac Larue- who are also named as executors.
Wit: Ly Harding, John Card and W.C. Middleton.

HAYNIE, JOHN.

June 10, 1803. August 13, 1803. Of Columbia Co. Georgia.
Wife: Mary, to have certain slaves, other slaves to be
sold and the money divided between 4 children, viz:
Peggy, Catherine, Malinda and Matilda. Money to be put
at interest until they come of age.
Exrs: wife, John Briscoe. Wit: James and Joshua Howard.

MITCHELL, DAVID.

July 10, 1803. 13 August, 1803.
Wife: Philomilla. Sons: John, James, David Dickerson
(to retain slaves now in their possession) and William.
Daughters: Sarah, Martha, Elizabeth and Mary, to have
1/4 of the slaves.
Exrs: wife, sons John, James and David D. Mitchell.
Wit: Nathaniel Tomlinson, James Trevas, William Porter.

BONNELL, ELIAS.

June 5, 1802. November 12, 1803.
Estate to wife Drusilla and daughters Nancy and Ellender.
Exrs: wife, Philander Smith.

DICK, JOHN.

November 1, 1800. November 6, 1803.
Legatee: Ann Foster, daughter of John and Mary Foster.
Exr: John Foster.

SMITH, CATHERINE.

November 6, 1803. February 27, 1804.
Daughters: Hannah, Rachel, Elizabeth, Margaret and Nancy,
each to have one silver dollar. Dau. Rachel to have spin-
ning wheel and clothes. Son: Martin, to have all remaining part of estate. Exrs: William Foster, John Grafton.
Wit: Thomas Grafton, John Winkell, Daniel McKnown.

COCHRANE, GEORGE.

April 3, 1803. August 13, 1803.
"To mother Sarah Cochrane- the desire of my heart is to
secure ample provision for the declining age of the best
of parents."Brothers: James and Hugh Cochrane.
Aunt Jane Little (relict of John Little, late of Penn.,
dec'd.), to have $100. annuity during life, to be remitt-
ed by brother Robert, to her daughters, $1000. to be di-
vided.To Jane Irwin (sister of John Irwin), of Brush
Creek, near Pittsburg, $500. A slave to Lucy Potter, dau.
of Ebenezer Potter of Virginia.A slave to god-daughter,
Maria Evans, dau. of Lewis Evans. Nephew, John Murdock,
only surviving child of sister Ann, dec'd. Mentions dear
father, William Cochrane and bro. William Cochrane, dec'd.
$1000. to be given the poor of Natchez.
Exr: brother Robert Cochrane.
Wit: John Rhea and William Flower.
(This will was written at New Orleans)

WOOD, SAMUEL.

September 1, 1802. 13 August, 1803.
Estate to be divided among children (not named).
Exrs: James McAfee, William Minor, Jr., Jeremiah Ruth.
Wit: Phil Love, John Boyle.

CONNELLY, PATRICK.

August 4, 1803. May 13, 1805.
Legatees: brothers and sisters, Darby, Margaret, Bridget, Mathais, Mary, Michael and Judy.
Exrs: Ferdinand Claiborne (merchant of Natchez), Jeremiah Routh and William Carey.
Wit: John Boyle and Charles McBride.
A codicil was added May 13, 1805, in which mention is
made of wife Priscilla, who had been provided for previously.

BERNARD, JOSEPH.

September 21, 1797. January 3, 1804.
Wife: Jane, who is entitled to some property that is
now in her mothers hands.
Children: Louisa, William, Joseph, Edward and unborn
child. Exrs: wife, William Dunbar, Esq., Robert Dunbar.
Wit: Charles Watrous, John Sullivan James Scott, M.D.,
Charles Anderson, William Moore, Hugh Davis, David Fer-
guson and Christopher Miller.

TROUTWINE, FREDERICK.

October 21, 1803.
Exr. and Legatee: John Harris.
Wit: J.W. Helaker, J.F. Keen.

WILLIAMS, JOHN.

Probated July 29, 1805.
Blacksmith. "To beloved wife Isabel, my cupboard, desk,
Windsor chairs and settee, her bed and bedding, table,
pots, pans and all kitchen furniture." Bros: Richard
and William. Exrs: wife, brother Richard.
Wt: James R. Rolling, Hugh Green, John Kerr.

TERRELL, MICAJAH.

Probated 30 October, 1805. Of North Carolina.
Wife: Hannah Terrell. Dau: Mary P. Terrell. Sons:
Archibald, Samuel, Timothy. Exr: son Timothy.
Wit: John Wray and Mathew Cozins.

JONES, ROBERT.

November 23, 1805, date of probate.
Mentions land purchased from James Brown, in Coatie
Bayou, near Red River, in Territory of Orleans.
Sister Mary Bowle's 3 sons, Thomas, Robert and Mathew
Bowles, and Betsy Holeman's son, Mathew Holeman, who
was born on my plantation in Sumner County, State of
Tennessee, on Station Camp Creek.
Daughters: Elizabeth and Effie Jones, to have a planta-
tion in Sumner Co., Tenn. Exr: brother Thomas Jones.
Wit: William Spiller, Job Routh, John Morford, John
Johnston.

FORD, JOSEPH.

November 6, 1804.
Wife: Rebecca Ford. Sons: John, Thomas, Joseph, Rob-
ert and George. Daughters: Esther Strawder and Eliz-
abeth Ford. Gr.children: George Holliway, Elizabeth
Ford. Exr: John Ford.
Wit: Robert Ford, John Spires, Jacob Gaice (?).

COREY, JEREMIAH.

Probated March 5, 1806.
Wife: Harriet Corey. Children: Mathew, Richard (now
an infant). Exr: brother Richard.
Wit: Elisha T. Hall, Gabriel Swayze, John C. Wickoof.

MCDUFF, ARCHIBALD.

May 9, 1803. ------ From the north of Ireland.
Sons: John and Patrick, to have land of my wife, Mary
Camobell. In case of decease of either son, surviving
one to have his share. Sons supposed to be living in
Antrim, Ireland. Exr: William Dunbar
Wit: Jonathan Roney and D. Dunbar.

ROSS, ALEXANDER.

----------July 1, 1806. Of the "Grange".
Legatees: estate to children of bro. James and sister
Ann; to Margaret Dunbar, dau. of my friend, William
Dunbar; nephew Alexander Ross, son of brother James;
John Kay, for faithful service.
Exr: friend William Dunbar, of "the Forest".
Wit: John Steele, John Brown, James Jones, Philander
Smith and Thomas Key.

WOOLDRIDGE, EDMOND.

June 15, 1807.
Wife: Isabella. Request that wife advise and consult
with her mother, Mrs. Hutchins, Col. Claiborne, Major
Bowman, as friends, relative to management of estate.
Exr: wife.   Wit: Cowles Mead, Ferdinand Claiborne
and Joseph Bowman. (Seal affixed at Whiteapple Village)

HIGDON, MARY.

August 8, 1805. Of the County of Jefferson, Miss. Ter.
Sons: Thomas Calvit, Joseph Calvit, Jeptha Higdon.
Exrs: sons Thomas and Joseph Calvit.
Wit: Edward Andrew, James Luckett, Hamilton Seton.

DORSEY, BENJAMIN.

9 August, 1807.
Wife: Nancy, to have 1/3 of estate.
Sons: Silas, to have plantation, Joab, to have a planta-
tion. Wit: Samuel Cooper, Mary Callahan, John Erwin.

HOLMES, SARAH.

November, 1800.
All of estate to son, Simpson Holmes.
Wit: Joshua Howard, Joseph Sessions, Jesse Hooper.

ELDERGILLS, JOHN.

2 November, 1807.
To Prosper King, 1000 acres of land in the Spanish Do-
minion of West Florida.
To Richard King, 1000 acres in the Spanish Dominion of
West Florida. "I leave unto Richard King 2/3 of $3280.
due me from the estate of Arthur Carney, amount now in
the Supreme Court of this Territory."
Wit: James Stewart, Daniel Greenleaf, Hezekiah Clark.
Exrs: Felix Hughes and Morris Custard.

GRAHAM, JOSEPH.

May 28, 1805. November 28, 1807.
Of New Geneva, Fayette Co., Penn. Legatees: brother
James Graham (youngest), bro. Thomas Graham.
Wit: John Ferrall, George Cammack, Alexander Sterling.

CAMPBELL, JOHN.

October 5, 1807. Late of Sommerset Co., Maryland.
Legatees: To sister Mary Campbell, dau. of Priscilla
Campbell alias Adams, of Sommerset Co., Maryland, land
in Territory of New Orleans. Half brother, Collin Adams,
to have land, also named as executor.

COOK, WILLIAM.

September 10, 1798.--------
Legatees: Solomon H. Wisdom, to have 500 acres of land
in Bayou Sara, bequeathed to me by John Mathews, his
will of record in Westmoreland Co., Penn., John Jackson. Exr: Solomon Wisdom.
Wit: Philander Smith, Thomas Jackson.

RAGAN, THOMAS.

Feb. 3, 1807. April 13, 1808. A carpenter.
Legatee: Hannah Hilton. Wit: Chandler Lindsley and
James Houston.

SHILLING, JACOB.

Jan. 12, 1805. April 13, 1808.
Wife: Mary, to have a plantation.
Sons: John, Abraham, Jacob and Matthew.
Daughters: Lorain, Barbara, Elizabeth, Anna, Mary.
Exrs: wife, Darius Anderson.
Wit: Samuel Boyd, Joseph Slocum, Darius Anderson.

WALKER, ANDREW.

February 15, 1808. April 13, 1808.
Of the town of Washington, formerly a Captain in the
Revolutionary Army, in Pennsylvania line.
Wife: Agnes.   Daughter: Charlotte Walker. "As I served
the United States as an officer in the Pennsylvania line
and thereby became a member of the Association of the
Cincinnati, in the State of Penn., I do hereby devise
and request all my interest and rights and advantages
in the funds of said Cincinnati and all priviledges and
advantages arising from the same, so far as she may be
capable of enjoying them, to said daughter Charlotte."
Exrs: friends Pierson Lewis, Robert H. Morrow.
Wit: James Hefferman, Asa W. Davis and David Wood.

SHILLING, PALSER.

March 31, 1808. May 21, 1808.
Col. John Steele and Roger Discon, to have all lands and

slaves for the benefit of daughter Mary.
Wit: William Cochrane, Daniel Grafton, Gabriel Tichenor.

BANKS, MARY.

June 21, 1805. May 2, 1808.
Originally of New Steafdford, Lincolnshire, Kingdom of
Great Britain.
Legatees: To niece, Sarah Susannah Banks, all of prop-
erty in America; S.S. Banks and nephew Robert Banks, pro-
perty in Great Britain; friend John Josse, Esq., Waltham
Abbey, Essex, Great Britain; Sarah Banks (sister-in-law).
Wit: Benjamin Farar, James Williams, Mary Farar.

FITZGERALD, GEORGE.

July 28, 1787. May 21, 1808.
Legatees: David Ross (friend), William Fitzgerald
(father), of Aberdeen, North Britain; brother James
Fitzgerald; sisters Barbara and Bella Fitzgerald.
Wit: Thomas Wilkin, D. Smith, John Montgomery, John
Girault, John Elder, Gill, William Gill.

MAHAN, SAMUEL S.

July, 1808. August 30, 1808.
Wife: Ann, now at Carlisle, Pennsylvania. Children:
Mary, John and David.
Exrs: Samuel Postlewaite, George Shiras, D. Mitchell,
Robert Moore. Probated by the order of Robert Moore.

MCLAUGHLIN, DUNCAN.

June 28, 1807. July Court, 1808.
Wife: mentioned, but not named.
Legatees: Catherine Black; sons: Dugal, Archibald
and Donald; daus: Margaret, Nancy, Flory, Mary.
Exrs: wife, son Dugald.
Wit: M. Gilchrist and Daniel Baugh.

WALCH, EDWARD.

January, 1808. July 15, 1808.
Wife and Exr: Unnamed
Wit: Mathew Cozins and Thomas McCrorey.

THIRY, JOHN BAPTISTE.

July 24, 1807. July, 1808.

Legatees: Jean Francis Thiry, Fere Jean Baptiste Thiry.
Exrs: Michael Fortier, David Urquhart, Armstrong Ellis.
(This will is written in French)

ELLIS, JOHN.

November 7, 1808. December, 1808.
Legatees: Wife, Sarah Ellis; children, Thomas and Mary
Ellis; father, Richard Ellis.
Exrs: wife, Abraham Ellis (bro.) and Thomas Percy.
Wit: Sam Brown, Ann Percy, Thomas Rodney.

KIRK, SUSAN.

October 3, 1808. January , 1809.
Exrs. and Legatees: James Kirk Cook (nephew) and William
Williams (hus. of late Susan Williams).
William Williams renounces executorship of Susan Kirk.

DILWORTH, JOSEPH.

July 21, 1808. January 7, 1809.
Brother William Dilworth, of Philadelphia, is named as
Executor. Daniel Elliott to take charge until brother
can arrive. Wit: James Pryor, Samuel Forsythe.

BOWMAN, CELESTE.

March 30, 1807.
(Late Celeste Hutchins).
Legatee and Exr: husband, Joseph Bowman, to have all es-
tate. Wit: John Linton, Thomas Harris, John Campbell,
James Lawler.

KELLEY, PATRICK.

July 20, 1809. 6 November, 1809.
Estate to relatives in Ireland.
Wit: Joshua Vail and James Johnston.

GLEN, SAMUEL.

October 11, 1809. Nov. 6, 1809.
Children: Sarah, Eliza and Jane Glen. 1/4 of estate
to be paid to Sarah Myars.
Exrs: Samuel Trigg, John Wood.
Wit: William Wilkinson and Pleasant Hunter.

GREEN, THOMAS.

Legatees: James Green (bro.), William Green (bro.),
father, Cowles Mead (bro.-in-law), Winn Sturgis to
have watch. Probated April, 1810.

PERRY, BARNABAS.

October 2, 1808. Nov. 1809.
Son: Barnabas Henry James Perry to have all of estate
and to be educated in best manner the country affords.
Wit: Alexander Montgomery, William H. King.
Exr: Jonathan Rucker.

REAGH, JOHN.

Jan. 2, 1810. Jan. 1810.
Wife: Susannah. Dau: Eliza.
Exrs: James Gormley, James McConnell.

EDMONONS, THOMAS.

Nov. 10, 1809.
To James and Mary Lennox, land in Natchez.
Wit: John Oldner, John Herrod and Armand De Vo.

MCKOUNS, DANIEL.

July 7, 1810. July, 1810.
Legatees: wife Susannah, little son James, bro. James
McKouns, sister Elizabeth Grafton.
Exrs: Thomas Grafton, William Barling, John McCaleb.
Wit: John Grafton, Sr., James McCowen.

COREY, RICHARD.

April 17, 1810. July 1810.
Wife: Prudence, children mentioned, but not named.
Exr: Nathan Luce.

HAMILTON, RICHARD.

To Rev. W. Stephen T. Badin, money to purchase catche
eisms to distribute gratis to the poor. Mentions
mother, brother and sister, but names not given.
Exrs. bro. Walter Hamilton, Clement Hill.
Will probated in Washington County, Kentucky.
(See Will Book "2"- 1808-1816)

WADE, JAMES.

Feb. 8, 1805.
Wife: mentioned, but not named.
Children: William and others.
Exrs: wife, Andrew Owens, Robert Turner.
Wit: Caleb Stovers, William Gibson, Robert Turner.

JOHNSON, FRANCIS.

17 May, 1802.------
Of Knox County, Indiana Territory.
$500. to Mrs Harvey, now residing at Judge Clarks, in
town of Vincennes. John Symes Harrison (legatee), son
of Governor Harrison. (Francis Johnson was Captain in
the 4th U.S. Regiment, stationed at Vincennes.)
Exr: William Henry Harrison (now Governor of Indiana Ter.)
Wit: John Campbell (Lt.in 2nd U.S. Reg.), W.R. Coupland,
and Daniel Carlin.

MCKIERNAN, CHARLES.

Oct. 27, 1810. Nov., 1810.
Legatees: "To Caroline and Elizabeth Stephenson, daus. of
Jonathan and Elizabeth Stephenson, $1000. each; rest of
estate to be used to establish a hospital.
Exrs: L. Baker and Samuel Postlewaite.

CURTIS, HANNAH.

May 29, 1802. April 14, 1807.
Children: Penelope, Mary, Hannah, Jeremiah, son Ephirams
(dec'd) children.
Exrs: Alexander Callender (son-in-law), Jeremiah Curtis
(son). Wit: Thomas Philips, Isarel Ecleman, John Jones.

REED, JULIAN.

Jan. 30, 1807. May 1807.
Legatees: Francis Reed (husband), Sarah Brown, Cather-
ine Brown. Exrs: Francis Reed and Charles Green.
Wit: John Linton, Walter McClelland, John M. Swindler.

SCOTT, JOHN.

May 14, 1801.------
Wife: Susan Scott. Children: Anabelle and John Scott.
Wit: Andrew Beall, Frederick Mann, Edward Beall.

WILLIS, JOHN.

April 21, 1802. June 12, 1802.
"Recently arrived from North Carolina after many dis-
appointments and difficulties."
Wife: Asenth. Children: mentioned, but unnamed.
Exrs: William C. Claiborne, Daniel Kerr.

SHUNK, WILLIAM.

May 7, 1802.----
Legatees: 3 sisters- Nancy, Polly and Sally, friend Jesse
Carter, who is partner in a cotton gin.
Exrs: Jesse Carter, Nehemiah Carter, Jr.
Wit: William Nicholls, Thomas Pollard, Isarel Smith.

JOHNSTON, DAVID.

Dec. 1, 1804. July, 1805.
Wife: Mary. Children: David (seven years of age) and
Ann (two years of age).
Exrs: wife, William Barland.
Wit: P. Connelly, William Hancock.

WILLIS, ASENTH.

Probated December, 1806.
Mentions seven younger children: John, William, Nancy,
Emily, Thomas, Daniel and Harriett. Sons-in-law:
William Dunbar, John Leybourne and William Voss.
Exrs: Elias Barnes, Samuel Bridges, John P. Willis.
Wit: Samuel Bridgers, Malcolm Currie, William T. Voss,
John Willis.

KENIONS, STEPHEN.

Dec.16, 1810. April, 1811.
Wife mentioned, but not named.
Wit: James McConnell, Ephiram Rulon, Charles F. Benden.

HUNT, ABIJAH.

June 3, 1811.
Brother Jeremiah Hunt to have $20, COO.
Exrs. and Legatees: bro. Jeremiah, William G. Forman,
David Hunt.

SIDEBOTTOM, JOHN.

Pro. October, 1810.
Legatee: Elizabeth Morris.
Wit: Robert A. Carter, William Thompson.

WHITEHEAD, WILLIAM.

Nov. 19, 1810. Nov. 1811.
Legatees: Alexander Bailee, and dau. of William Voss.
Exr: William Voss.
Wit: Ransom Searcy, Peter Terrell.

GAILLARAL, ISAAC.

July 3, 1811. August, 1811.
Legatees: children of Elizabeth Kilgore(wife of Benj.);
god-dau. Nancy Ellis ; numerous nieces and nephews.
Plantation of 1300 acres not to go out of the family.
Exrs: Benjamin Farrar and John Taylor.
Wit: Augustus A. Grieve, Kerbe Goolshe.

PANNILLS, JOSEPH.

November 30, 1809. October, 1811.
Children: Joseph Bonapart, David, Alexander Washington,
Octavia Obedience. Wife to have use of furniture during
her life and $5500 per year, but furniture, stock and
slaves not to be sold.
Exrs: son David, James Williams, Capt. Benj. Farrar,
Col. John Steele.
Wit: Daniel Linton, John Taylor.

HUTCHINS, ANN.

March 11, 1811. Nov. 16, 1811.
To dau. Mary Green (wife of Abner Green), slaver.
To dau. Elizabeth Brooks (wife of William Brooks), slaves.
To dau. Ann McDurmot (wife of Bryant McDurmot), slaves.
Gr.daughter: Magdalin Claiborne (dau. of Virginia and
Ferdinand Claiborne). Isabelle Charlotte Claiborne (wife
of Thomas Claiborne). Sons: John and Samuel Hutchins.
Friend Joseph Bowman; gr.son Robert Hutchins Bowman,
(son of Celeste Bowman, dec'd), Joseph Bowman, father
of Robert Hutchin Bowman, to take charge of son's prop-
erty. Exrs: son John and Joseph Bowman.
Wit: Robert Westcott,I. Linton, B. Seamans.

DOYLE, MARTIN.

Feb.5, 1811. October, 1813.
Slaves to have their freedom. All estate to Daniel
Fowler and Solomon Swayne, who are named as Exrs.
Wit: George Daughtery, T. Jackson.

SEAMENS, BENJAMIN.

April 10, 1812. May 23, 1812.

Legatees: sisters, Susanna Alney, Sarah Spragin, Martha
Newell; bros: Pres, William, Benjamin Seamen, Benjamin
Newell (son of Springfield Newell).
Exrs: Samuel Postlewaite, Joseph Bowmar (residing in Adams
Co.), Paul Fearing (residing in Muskingum, Ohio.).

BROOKS, E.M.C.

October 12, 1812.
$1000 to go to the Roman Catholic Church of the city of
Natchez, Miss. Rest of estate to daus. Ann Eliza Claiborne
Brooks and Charlotte Maria Brooks, in case of the death
of daughters, property to go to husband, William Brooks.
Exrs: husband, John Hutchins, Ferdinand Claiborne, Joseph
Bowman. Bryan McDermott to act as guardian to said daus.
Wit: D. Lattimore, T. Mangunn.

NAURCHERE, MARGARET.

August 18, 1812. Nov. 21, 1812.
Sally Nauchere (dau. of son Joseph), to have estate.
Slave Agatha to have her freedom.

ROSE, ENOCH.

October, 1810. Nov. 21, 1812.
Wife: Mary Rose. Sons: Enoch and Philip Rose.
Daughters: Polly Rose, Abia O--- (?), Betty Herryman,
Jemina Slatter, each to have $1.
Wit: Robert Turner, Patrick Toland.

ELLIS, MARY.

Nov. 4, 1806.
Gr.daus: Mary Farrar and Ann Eliza Farrar, to have slaves.
Exr: Benjamin Farrar.

MATHEWS, GEORGE.

October 24, 1806. April 5, 1813.
Daughters: Rebecca Merriwether and Jane Telfair, 2400
acres of land in Kentucky, part of a 4000 acre survey,
where H. Roads lives. Grandsons: George, Archer and
John M. Mathews (sons of John Mathews), to have 1000
acres of land in Ohio.Gr.sons: George, Francis Merriwether, Charles L. and Samuel Mathews (sons of William
Mathew). Wife: Mary, to have all property I received
with her in marriage, 2 negroes and other slaves, my
gold watch and chain.
Exrs: George and Charles Mathews.

MCCARY, JAMES.

16 February, 1813.
Legatees: Thomas Irwin (son of friend "alter Irwin),
Thomas Harrison, ---Curtis (friends), negro girls Sally
and Franky, to have their freedom.
Exr: Walter Irwin.

HUTCHINS, SAMUEL.

Feb. 10, 1810. Feb. 4, 1812.
Legatees: Magdaline Claiborne (sister), wife of Gen. Fer-
dinand Claiborne; Mary Mead (sister), wife of Cowles Mead,
to have $1000.: Anthony McDermott (son of Bryant McDermott
; Anthony White Hutchins (son of bro. John Hutchins); Ann
and Charlotte Brooks (daus. of William and Elizabeth Brooks
; Virginia Claiborne (only dau. of Ferdinand and Magdaline
Claiborne). Exr: Ferdinand Claiborne.

ROBBS, MARY.

Oct. 13, 1807. October Court, 1807.
Children: Nicholas, Matgaret (2 eldest), John, Peter and
Elizabeth. Exrs: John and Peter (sons).
Wit: Isarel Smith and Michael Brewer (?).

FULTON, HENRY.

September 4, 1813. ------- From Allegeheny Co., Penn.
Exrs: John King (of Beaver Co., Penn) and Henry Fulton(
of Allegeheny Co. Penn.)
Wit: Edward Goldman, John Manson.

All estate to mother, Mary Clark, of Germantown, Penn.
Exrs: Richard Relf and Beverly Chew. (This will is a
copy of will probated in New Orleans)

WILKINS, THOMAS.

February, 1792.   Feb. 1812.
Legatees: Bernard Lintot, John Murdock, each to have
100 pounds in sterling money, Daniel Clark, Jr. to have
all my wearing apparel. Exrs: Daniel Clark, Jr. and
Bernard Lintot. Wit: John O'Conner, G. Cocharne and D.
Ferguson.

GUILE, JACOB.

Probated February, 1812.
Legatees: family, but does not name them.
Exrs: Joseph Forman and asa Goodman.

FEATHERSTONE, WILLIAM.

April 9, 1812. July, 1812. Attorney, of Henderson County,
Kentucky. Wife: Martha A. Featherstone.
Exrs: wife, Meredith Fisher.

GORE, DAVIS.

February 28, 1812. July, 1812.
Town of Washington, Adams Co. Miss. Ter.
Wife: Pamelia, to have house and land.
Daughter: Nancy Curtis, wife of John Curtis.
Exrs: wife, John Curtis.
Wit: Thomas Downing, Philip A. Engle, A.H. Holmes.

CERRES, GABRIEL.

16 June, 1810------
(Will is written in French)

STEELE, JOHN.

Jan. 31, 1818. Jan. 1819.
Of city of Natchez, and a native born citizen of Virginia. Legatees: nephew Robert Alexander, to have $6000.
in money; Charles Brownlee, of Kentucky, to have $6000
in money; brother James and his four daughters, $400.
each; brother William Steele and his children; sister
Janet; a large number of slaves to have their freedom.

Exrs: Robert Alexander, Samuel Postlewaite, John Taylor, James Wilkins (executers for that part of estate
which is in Miss. and La.) Exrs: William Steele, Robert Steele, William Steele, Jr. (Exrs. for estate in
Kentucky.

OSMUN, BENJAMIN.

May 27, 1815. July 11, 1815.
Legatees: Osmun Claiborne, son of General Ferdinand
Claiborne, Magdaline Claiborne (widow of Gen. F. Claiborne)
and other children of Gen. Claiborne, John Taylor.
Exrs: Philander Smith, William Wright, John Taylor.

MINOR, MAJOR STEPHEN.

October 23, 1815. Jan. 8, 1816.
Wife: Katherine, to have real and personal estate. Men-
tion is made of money wife had received from her father,
Bernard Lintot. Daughters: Frances, Katherine Lintot
Minor. Sons: Stephen, William, John. To the surviving
children of Thomas Powers (or Powell), a large tract of
land in Louisiana. Exrs: wife, brother John Minor.
Wit: Lyman Harding, Sarah Powell.

DUNBAR, WILLIAM.

October 30, 1810
Wife: Dinah, to have electrical machine and microscope
and other instruments of superior value.
Daughters: Elizabeth and Helen, to have land where Evan
Shelby lives. Isarel Smith to have trust for Polly Doan
and her children. Son: William, to have all chemical, as-
tronimical, philosophical apparatus, hoping he will make
good use of them. Daughters: Ann, Margaret, Eliza, Helen,
are bequeathed the salt works. Exrs: wife, Samuel Postlewaite.

ANDREU, JAYME.

Feb. 28, 1820.
Codicil to will of Jayme Andreu.
Legatee: Clary Quegles.
Wit: Woodson Wren, William Cathcart, B. D. Bourdan.

TAYLOR, ROBERT

Oct. 19, 1819.
Sons: William, Windsor, James and John.
Exrs: John McCaleb, John Pipes, Isaac Taylor.
Wit: Robert Turner, Augustus Taylor.

AGAR, ROBERT

July 14, 1819.
Of Cambridge, Mass. Wife, Margaret, to have estate for
life, then to 3 children of bro. Peter Agar, of London,.
England, and Julia Whitmore, when she reaches the age of
21 years.
Exr: James Rule, of Cambridge, Mass.
Wit: Samuel Worcester, Marsh Hanbery, Zachariah Barker.

BINGAMAN, LEWIS

OCT. 19, 1819.
Legatees: George Denshire Banks, Robert Sutton Banks
(nephews); Eliza Walker (niece) ; children of Adam Bingaman. Exrs: Francis Surget, John Brickwood Taylor,
Wit: Alexander C. Henderson, Thomas Henderson.

RICHARDS, SAMUEL B.

June 28, 1817.
Legatees: Augustus, William and James (nephews-sons
of bro. William) ; John Caldwell Richards (son of brother John).
Exrs: John Richards (brother), John Taylor.
Wit: A.H. Buckholts, Isaac Overaker, John G.W. Buckholts, James T. Magruder, Jr.

WHITE, JOHN HAMPTON

Oct. 12, 1819.
Wife: Jane White. Cousins: Susan Chetwood, Sarah Jeff
(both of Elizabethtown, N.J.); Elizabeth Carson, of Pa.;
John B. Lawerence, of New York.
Exrs: wife, Daniel E. Elliott.
Wit: Lyman Harding, John Hankimon, C. Hysinger.

COLEMAN, JEREMIAH

July 14, 1817.
Wife: Pharobah Coleman. Children: Isaiah, Jeremiah,
Johnathan, Asa, Stephen, Silas, Penelope, Phebe, Susanna,
Lydia and Anne.

Exrs: wife, son Isaiah, bro. Isarol Coleman.
Wit: William L. Chew, George F. Wilkinson.

CARAVAXAL, FRANCISCO

March 10, 1818.
Wife: Elizabeth. Son: Francisco. Dau: July Ann.
Exr: wife. Wit: Joseph Galvan, ----Quegles, Domingo
Garcia, James Willis.

STANDARD, HUGH

Dec. 25, 1819.
Wife: Ann Standard.
Exrs: wife, White Turpin. Wit: G. Pearce, Lewis Winston,
James McAllister.

PALESKE, CHARLES

August 17, 1820.
Estate to mother, Hannah Paleske, at her decease to sister,
Maria Wilhemina Paloske. Exr: James Chambers.
Wit: G.S. Hollyday, J.W. Carvill, D. Chambers.

OVERAKER, GEORGE

August 17, 1816.
Legatees: wife Margaret; bro. Isaac Overaker; neice of
wife, Elizabeth Patton; Lewis Evans, trustee for daus.
Elizabeth Tichenor and Maria Overaker.
Exr: wife. Wit: John Hankinson, H. W. Huntington,
Horace N. Huntington.

DANGERFIELD, WILLIAM

June 22, 1820.
Estate to mother, Elizabeth Dangerfield, for life, then
to brothers and sisters. Exr: mother.
Wit: J.H. McComas, Sturges Sprague, Charles N. Norton,
Thomas M. Gildart.

NELSON, PETER

Dec. 19, 1812.
Legatees: wife, Margaret; Margaret Sharbino; Mary Craven;
Anne Taylor; Sarah Clark; Magdaline Holbrook; sons, Marson and Peter, Jr. ; dau. Catherine. Exrs: 3 above mentioned children. Wit: Daniel Whitaker, Stephen Dunn.

GILBERT, JAMES

October 19, 1818.
Estate to mother, Nancy Gilbert and brothers and sisters
(not named). Exr: Thomas Gilbert.
Wit: Thomas Foster, Sr. and Thomas Gilbert.

DORMAN, ELIZABETH

May 2, 1819.
Daughter: Margaret Allen.
Exrs: Samuel Postlethwaite and William Baker.
Wit: John Jaylambs and William Thompson.

SWAYZE, NATHAN

May 9, 1819.
Legatees: wife Ann ; son Nathan ; dau. Lydia; widow
and heirs of son David, dec'd.
Exrs: son Nathan, Daniel Rawlings.
Wit: Thomas Eaton, W.B. Fowles, William Daugharty.

FLEMMING, JOHN

March 22, 1819.
Legatees: John G. Flemming, Thomas Flemming, John G.
and Horatio Flemming (cousins); brother Robert Flemming
(of Rowan Co., N.C.) ; Samuel Flemming; Margaret, Mary
and Rebecca Freeland ; Nancy and Elizabeth Brawley;
Moses T., David F., James G. Flemming.
Exrs: Thomas Flemming and William D. Baker.
Wit: A. Terrell, R.M. Green, Dinah Flemming.

SPENCER, JOHN

June 1, 1819. July, 1819.
Legatee: Abraham Defiance.
Sworn to by Richard Sessions and Mathew R. Fenton.
Nuncupative will.

TIERNAN, PETER

October 8, 1818
Legatee and Exr: Lydia Tiernan (wife).
Wit: D. Lattimore, Samuel Thornberry, Jr., Benjamin Zane.

MC INTYRE, HUGH.

Nov. 13, 1819.

Legatees: bro. John of Worthington, England ; bro.
Lexander of Edinburgh ; sister Mary, near Fortwilliam,
Scotland. Exrs: John Henderson, George Ralston, Henry
Postlethwaite. Wit: Horace F. Walworth, Aaron T. Melick,
Thomas Spalding.

HOSMER, LYDIA

Nov. 13, 1819.
Legatees: stepdau., Ann B. Hosmer, provided she survives
Lydia Hosmer, otherwise estate to lawful children of
brother Johnathan Robbins, of Watertown, Mass.; sister,
Mrs. Ann Faulkner, of Biblica, Mass. ; Miss Martha Robbins,
of Watertown, Mass. ; Louis Carter, of Miss.
Exr: Amos Whiting, of Gibson Port, Miss.
Wit: James E. Hart, George R. Williams, Clara Garnier.

BREWER, SAMUEL

Sept. 5, 1819.
Legatees: bros. Robert and William Brewer, of New Jersey,
and John Glover (partner).
Exrs: George R. Williams and John Corn.   Wit: Robert Cole,
T. Baker and Thompson Gardner.

BLACK, BENJAMIN

Nov. 6, 1819.
Legatee: John Black (son).
Wit: William Murray, John Camp Thomas Kees.

BRUNE, FREDERICK

May 22, 1819. Nov. Court, 1819.
Estate to mother, or in case of her death, to 3 sisters,
Christina Sophia Margarita (wife of Joseph Pullim),
Joanna Sophia Fredrika, Wilhemina.
Exr: William Brune (brother), in case of absence George
Ralston and Dr. William E. Lehman.
James Ferguson swore in court that he saw Fred. Brune
execute this will. Mother and sisters live in Iserlohm,
in Westphalien Province, Russia.

BAILLE, ALEXANDER

July 19, 1819.
Was in service of Mexican Republican Army.
Heirs not named. Exrs: Anthony Campbell, Philo Nichols.
Wit: Bank Wakeman, Joseph B. Howell, William Cullen.

COX, JOHN C.

Dec. 15, 1816. Feb. 15, 1817.
Legatees: Wife and children. Not named.
Nuncupative will. Taken down by Robert Williams at the
death bed of John Cox.

CLAIBORNE, ISABELLA C.H.

April 15, 1816.
Legatees: Dr. Thomas A. Claiborne (husband), Charlotte
Claiborne (niece), Hutchins and Ferdinand Claiborne (nep-
ews), Magdaline Claiborne (sister).
By codicil, freedom to Sarah, a slave.
Exrs: Lyman Harding (attorney).
Wit: D.F. Harris, Alexander Calvit and Anne Green.

CARSON, JOSEPH

April 18, 1817. May 12, 1817.
Legatees: Charlotte (wife) and unborn infant; son James
Green Carson; natural daughter by Mrs. Johnson, of Pas-
cagoula, formerly Patsey Brewer.
Exrs: James Green (bro.-in-law), wife (Caroline Charlotte
Carson). Wit: William Baldwin, Robert Caller, L. George
Buchanan.

CRAWFORD, WILLIAM

Oct. 9, 1817. Nov. 2, 1817.   Of Green County, Pennsylvania.
Oldest children to go to Alexander Miller, Steubenville,
Ohio. Youngest children to Mrs. Weeks.
Exrs: Christopher Rankin and Henry Postlethwaite.
Not signed, attested to by James Carrel.

CARTER, JESSE

Feb. 8, 1816.
Legatees: Samuel Postlewaite, as trustee for daughter,
Lydia; George Poindexter, Jr. (gr.son); daughter Eliza
Trask, wife of Isarel Trask.
Exrs: Isarel E. Trask and daughters, Eliza and Lydia.
Wit: Lyman Harding, William Walters, Isaac Carter.

GREEN, ABNER

July 19, 1809.
Wife: Mary Green.   Sons: James and William.
Daughters: Elizabeth Celeste, Charlotte Caroline and

Anne Magdaline and Maria. Exr: wife.
Wit: Louis Dulseckey, Joseph Collins, Joseph Bowman.

TOMLINSON, ELIZABETH

August 6, 1816
Legatees: James T. Baker (gr. son), son of William D.
Baker; John I. and William D. Baker, sons of John I. Baker;
John I. Baker (son); James Mitchell (nephew).
Exr: John I. Baker.
Wit: Alexander Sanderson, Jacob Heater, James Buford,
William Reid.

DEAN, SETH

Dec. 27, 1815. August 16, 1816.
Wife: Polly. Legatees: wife; dau. Elizabeth and heirs;
children of brother James Dean.
Left 4000 acres of British grants and 70,000 acres of
Yazoo Lands. Exrs: wife, Price and Parke Walton. Wit:
Hezekiah Kibboe, Daniel Boyce and John Hughes.

DAVIS, JOSHUA

May 13, 1816.
Legatees: wife Sarah: Betsy, Sarah, Polly, Nancy (daus.);
Gardiner, Thomas, Redden, James, Seth, Martin (sons).
Exrs: wife, Thomas Ford (friend).
Wit: Daniel Fowler, Duncan McMillan, John P. Guvinau.

DURATY, WILLIAM

August 25, 1811.
Legatee: Rebecca Bignal (friend), also named executrix.
Wit: Job Routh, Isaac Burley, William Evans, F.L. Turner.
Proven by the oath of Job Routh.

ELLIS, ABRAM

March 2, 1816.
Legatees: Nancy Butler (dau.); Richard Ellis (son);
John Ellis Duncan and Sarah Duncan (gr. children); slaves
Louisa and dau. Bet to be given freedom.
Exrs: Benjamin Farrar (in case of his death, Theodore Stark),
Thomas Butler, son Richard- when he reaches 21 years.
Wit: William C. Conner, W.D. Baker, Thomas Eaton.

FOREMAN, JOSEPH

June 25, 1816.
Discharge engagements to estate of late brother, Col.
Joseph (?) Foreman, of Baltimore, also draft to Thomas
Irwin.   Exrs: Wife, Catherine Remsen Foreman and her
brother, Jacob Remsen Holmes.
Wit: I.M. Hunt, White Turpin.

GLASSBURN, GODFREY

July 13, 1815. October, 1817.
Legatees: wife, Lavina, and unborn child; friend Mrs. Re-
becca Fletcher (wife of Capt. Richard Fletcher)
Exr: wife.   Wit: C.N. Read, John Forsythe, I.I. Fletcher.

HULL, DANIEL

August 7, 1817. Oct. 30, 1817.
Brother Charles Hull (of New York) to distribute estate
to nearest friends, as he sees fit; reserving to himself
his proper share.
Exrs: James C. Wilkins, Abraham M. Feltus, Chancey Pettibone.   Wit: Levi Purnell, James Ferguson, Josiah Morris.

KERCHEVAL, JAMES

Nov. 23, 1814. Nov. 22, 1817.
Wife: Susan, dau. of Stephen Minor.
Exrs: Maj. Stephen Minor, wife
Wit: Lyman Harding, F. Scip, Willman Lehman.

LAPE, JOHN

October 23, 1817.
Wife: Susannah.   Children: Christiana, William and
Agnes Maria.
Exrs: Thomas Munce, Abraham Scrantorn, wife Susannah.
Wit: Jacob Fry, William B. Cowan.

LONG, JACOB.

Sept. 8, 1817. Nov. 22, 1817.
Legatees: sister Elizabeth Long and Mrs. Martha Long.
Exr: John H. Robinson.
Wit: Sally Vandern, Martha Long, John Robinson

LACAZE, BERNARD

March 22, 1815. August 16, 1816.
Legatees: Nancy, widow of Frederick Veuve and her dau.

Elizabeth. Exr: Nancy Veuve.
Wit: John Felix Daller, Alex Baille, J. Whitehurst.

MARTIN, CHARLES

June 21, 1817. July 15, 1817.
Legatees: Relatives in Ireland.
Sworn to as substance of will of Charles Martin by Dr.
Fred Seip, attending physician. Was a clerk on a steam
boat. Exr: John Lombard.

THOMAS, MATHEW

Oct. 14, 1817. Nov. 22, 1817.
Brother Greenbury Thomas to hold the estate in trust for
family of Mathew Thomas.
Sworn to as substance of will by H. Tooley, physician.
Exr: Greenberry Thomas (brother).

GARCIA DE Texada, Garcia

Oct. 14, 1818. Nov. 22, 1818.
Legatees: Roman Catholic Church, New Orleans; Roman
Catholic congregation of Natchez, provided they or-
ganize in 2 years, otherwise to trustees of Hospital
there; wife Mechale; sons John and Joseph.
Exrs: son Joseph and Leonard Pomet.
Wit: A. Campbell, Gerome Sarpy, Marale Pomet.

FITZGERALD, JAMES.

May 9, 1816.
Legatees: Executor to manage property for three child-
ren until youngest comes of age .
Exr: William Crawford. Nuncupative will.

BROOKS, SAMUEL

August 13, 1812.
Legatees: Dau. Dolly Newman, wife of Joseph Newman; dau.
Betsy Hutchins, wife of John Hutchins; children of the
above mentioned daughters.
Exrs: John Hutchins (son-in-law), Samuel Postlethwaite.
Wit: I. Thompson, I. Taylor, I. Bigelow.

HUSTON, JAMES

May 30, 1817. March 30, 1818.
Wife Hannah, to have estate during her life, after her

decease to brother William 1/3 and sister Jane 1/3, wife
to dispose of balance.
Exrs: wife, Robert Turner.
Wit: Robert Turner, John Pipes.

DONNANT, DENNIS FRANCOIS

Dec. 14, 1812.
Wife: Marie Therese. Sister, Mll. Donnant.
Will made in Paris, written in French.

BATHOS, JOHN.

March 26, 1818. April 6, 1818.
Children: Anne Maria, Mary Ann, Julian Ann Bathos.
Exrs: Elijah Smith, Peter Little, Leonard Pomet.
Wit: Charles B. Green, Eustus French.

ANDREU, JAYME

June 17, 1818.
Legatees: Miss Maria Pomet; brothers, Salvator and Ignasio
Andreu.   Wit: E. Turner, Christopher Miller, B. Bourdin.
Exrs: Joseph Quegles, Batista Gual, Francisco Goncadella.
Copied by Wooden Wren, Clerk of Adams County, at request
of Jayme Andreu.

ENGLE, PHILIP

Nov. 13, 1817. June 29, 1818.
Wife and Exr: Mary Engle.
Wit: H. Tooley, V. Robitaille, D. Lattimore.

MCINTOSH, JAMES

Nov. 18, 1809.
Legatees: David and James Williams (nephews), Mary G. Urquhart and Anna Williams (nieces). Each of children of
my sister by second marriage. Mother to have bequest and at
her death to children of sister by first marriage.
Exrs: mother, David Urquhart, Thomas Urquhart (of New Orleans).

MCINTOSH, WILLIAM

May 6, 1800.
Legatees: Mother to have estate for life, then bro. James
McIntosh. Exrs: William Dunbar, James McIntosh.
Wit: William Glascock, Robert Gibson.

WILLS, ELIAS

April 11, 1818.   July, 1818.
Exr: wife Ann Wills.
Wit: Joseph Brandt, Charles Moore.

KARR, JOSEPH

Sept. 13, 1813.   July, 1818.
Exr. and Legatee: Josiah Hendon (friend).
Wit: Absalom Sharp, John E. Bennett, Josiah Buford.

STERNE, PEYTON

May 11, 1818.   Jan. 1819.
Legatees: 3 colored children, sons and daughter of a cer-
tain woman of color, Milly.
Exrs: David Lawson, Absalom Sharp.
Wit: Alex. Baille, John Dickson, Jr., David Lawson.

STEELE, JOHN

Dec. 31, 1818.   Jan. 1819.
Legatees: Robert Alexander (nephew); bro. James and 4 daus:
Charles Brownlee, of Kentucky; brother William Steele and
heirs; brother Robert Steele and heirs; sister Janet Alexander.   Exrs: Robert Alexander, Edward Turner, Samuel
Postlethwaite, John Taylor, James C. Wilkins, for property
in Mississippi and Louisiana. William and Robert Steele,
Robert Steele, Jr., Peter Alexander, for property in Kentucky
and Virginia.

MC CRACKEN, GEORGE

14----, 1819.
Legatees: Sally Butler, a free woman of color, Sally a
negro girl to be emancipated.
Exrs: Walter Irvine, Thomas Munce. Wit: A. Scranton, Jr.,
Samuel Patterson, Jacob Fry, James Hacket.

SEIP, FREDERICK

Dec. 5, 1818.
Wife, Anna, to provide for the family and to raise and
educate Mary A. Shields, bro. Peter Seip, son John Seip.
Exrs: wife, Andrew McCrery. Wit: John Kerr, John Lombard,
John Richard. Brother Peter Seip, of Philadelphia.

WILLIAMS, ISAAC

Dec. 11, 1812. April 1, 1816.
Legatees: Elizabeth Salth and Mary Williams (sisters),
residing in Brandy Parish, Pembrokeshire, South Wales.
Testator late a soldier in his Majesty's 1st regiment
of Guards, now a weaver.
Exrs: James McIntosh and David Urquehart.
Wit: Winthrop Sargent, Mary S. Allen, Drury Suggs.

GILBERT, CHRISTINE

Oct. 8, 1815. Jan. 8, 1816.
Legatees: Mother, all brothers and sisters equally.
Exrs: Samuel Postlethwait and Henry Postlethwait.
Wit: Joel Nowell, Isarel Smith, John Robb, Walter
Skillman and Joshua Davis.

ALEXANDER, ISAAC

August 1, 1817.
Sons: Amos, Thomas, John, William, Isaac, Jacob, Abraham.
Dau: Rebecca.
Exrs: Archibald Terrell, Richard Sessions (friends), Amos,
Thomas (sons). Wit: Hardy Sojourner, Joshua Howard, Jr.,
Canady Cason. Proven by the oath of Hardy Sojourner.

ADAMS, PHILIP

Oct. 23, 1817. Nov. 22, 1817. Of Virginia.
Legatee: George Adams (father).
Exr: John H. Robinson. Wit: John Buckley, W.S. Winn
and Thomas Anderson.

BARLAND, WILLIAM

Nov. 1, 1817. Nov. 22, 1817.
Wife: Fanny. Son: William and unborn child.
Exrs: William Barnard, Joseph Barnard, Jonathan Stoker.
Wit: William Barnard, Zachariah H. Dorsey, J. Taylor.

BURGET, JOHN

October 13, 1817.
Legatee: Mary Hutchinson (friend).
Exrs: Samuel Patterson and Walter Irvine.
Wit: James Hacket, Ebenezer Clapp, A.B. Salisbury, Rob-
ert Fagen. Proven by the oath of James Hacket and
Robert Fagen.

HART, J.E.

June 28, 1823. July 28, 1823.
Legatees: mother; sister Hannah: children of brother
John A. Hart (dec'd.), James P. and John L. Hart;
bro. Gideon Hart and bro. Thomas Hart.
Exrs: brother Gideon Hart (of Ohio), John Perkins, Esq.,
Thomas Coit.
Wit: W.G.Parker, Samuel Gustoni, H.F. Walworth.

BARLAND, WILLIAM

June 19, 1811. April, 1818.
"Whereas on the 7th day of April, 1789, in presence of
James Stodart, W.Bainor, John Short, I did purchase my
freedom and companion, Elizabeth Barland, and three in-
fant children, called Andrew Barland, Elizabeth Barland,
Jr. and Margaret Barland, of James Eilers." (long will)
Exrs: sons Andrew, James, William and son-in-law William
Henderson.

HOGATT, WILFORD.

May 27, 1814. April 1, 1816
Wife: mentioned, but not named.
Children: Nathaniel, Fanny, Willford, Mary, Eliza, Jane,
James and Agnes. Exr: friend John Wood.

CARTER, NEHEMIAH.

March 3, 1814. April, 1814.
Of Wilkinson County, Indian Territory.
Children: son Parsons (of Louisana), son Isaac (youngest),
son Jesse, daughters, Hannah Palmer, Phebe Phipps, Sally
Hackett. 3 children of daughter Betsy Adams.
Exr: son Jesse. Wit: Isarel Smith, William Waters.

TOOLEY, ADAM.

May 26, 1813. April, 1814.
Wife: Hannah, to have land, furniture and slaves.
Sons: James, Henry and Bryan. Daughter: Henrietta Bryan.
Mentions kindess and attention shown his family by his
son-in-law, John W. Bryan.
Exrs: sons James and Henry, son-in-law John W. Bryan.
Wit: Frederick Beard, Andrew Richards, Susannah Richards.

BESANTE, HERNANDEZ.

Probated July, 12, 1814. Mother: Andrea. Exr: Pedro Galle-
lay (brother-in-law).

SWAYZE, GABRIEL.

Sept. 29, 1814. October Court, 1814.
Wife: Lydia.
Sons: Lewis and Ambrose. Daughters: Rebecca (wife of
Robert Holmes), Euphany, Catherine, Elinor and Mary
Briner (step-dau.). Exrs: wife, Nathan Swayze, Jr.
Wit: Henry Noble, Eleuzer Howell, Gabriel Swayze, Jr.

TRIGGS, WILLIAM.

June 11, 1813. Oct. 25, 1813.
Wife: Rachel. Son: William King.
Legatees: Daniel Connelly, Lilbun L. Henderson.
Exrs: L.L. Henderson (of Abingdon, Va.) and John L.
Trigg (now at Saltville).
Wit: P. Boltzill, William James, John Lewis.

HUNT, HENRY.

July 27, 1814. 23 Sept., 1814.
Legatees: Keziah Ash (friend), William Hunt (bro.), R.H.
Morris, Philip A. Engel, G. Glasburn.

GILDART, FRANCIS.

June 2, 1812. Oct. 3, 1814.
Wife: Sophia and children (not named).
Exrs: wife and her bro. Theodore Stark.
Wit: H. Tooley and James Tooley.
(Francis Gildart from Tennessee)

TILTON, NEHEMIAH.

Late of Delaware. August 22, 1814. October 3, 1814.
Mention is made of 4 children, but only son Nehemiah
named.Exrs: son Nehemiah, William Shields, White Turpin. Wit: Theodore Stark, David Harry, Benjamin Osmun.

GUSTIN, RICHARD.

Feb. 22, 1812. December, 1814.
Legatees: mother; sisters Maria and Jane; bro. Samuel.
Exrs: Samuel Postlewaite and brother Samuel Gustin.
Wit: Charles B. Green.

MURRAY, ALEXANDER.

July 5, 1812. December, 1814.

Legatees: mother, Catherine Murray (living in the north of Ireland); sisters, Rebecca Murray, Mary Hammond (wife of William Hammond).
Wit: J. Lintot, James Kempe, Robert Scott.
Alex. Murray, late of Pennsylvania.

DAINGERFIELD, HENRY.

Probated. 21 Jan., 1815·
Wife: Elizabeth, named as executrix.   Children: William, Henry, Edward and Mary·
Wit: David Holmes, W. Turpin, Park Walton·

MARTEL, PAUL.M.L.

March 20, 1815.
Consul of France to United States, residing in Natchez.
Legatees: slaves to have their freedom; friend John Sarade (or Jarade); Eliza Deme, dau. of widow Deme, of Natchez.   Exr: Fielding L. Turner (of City of New Orleans).   Wit: Alexander Baillee, F.L. Turner, F· Sarrade.

MITCHELL, PHILOMILLA.

Probated January 28, 1821.
(Widow of David Mitchell)· Children: David D. Mitchell, Sarah Mitchell and Martha Erwin.
Exrs: son David, brother Philander Smith, friend William Barker (or Broker).

DUNBAR, ROBERT.

Probated January 10, 1826.
Daughters: Jane Ferguson, Charlotte Newman, Elizabeth Benoist (?) (eldest daughter). Sons: William (eldest), James, Joseph, Samuel, Isaac and Robert.
Exrs: sons James, Joseph and Samuel.
Wit: John Branch and John W. Monete(?).

Allen, Bennett -- Elizabeth Rabb, Oct. 3, 1800
(Not recorded in this office)

Bradley, James -- Polly Oglesby, Dec. 23, 1802
(Recorded in Book 1 -page 1)

Claiborne, F.S. -- Magdaline Hutchins, Aug. 19, 1802
(Not recorded in this office)

Copeland, Jesse -- Polly Brown, Dec. 30, 1802
(Recorded in Book 1, p. 1

Duncan, Abner -- Esther Eldridge, June 24, 1799
(Not recorded in this office)

Davis, Robert -- Mary Nicholson, June 3, 1801

Davidson, Thomas -- Mary Kinnerd, June 30, 1803

De Santa, Hosa -- Polly Hooper, July 23, 1800

Ellis, John -- Sarah Piercy, Feb. 22, 1800

Fisher, Elias -- Mary Leinhart, Oct. 17, 1801

Harwick, James -- Patsey Ellis, Feb. 22, 1801

King, Jesse -- Sophia McKinley, Jan. 8, 1801

McGinty, John -- Sophey James, June 17, 1800

McCullough, John M. -- Susannah Jackson, Sept. 3, 1802

McDermatt, Bryan -- Ann Hutchinns, July 25, 1799

Nolan, Philip -- Francis Lintot, Dec. 19, 1799

Qegles, Joseph -- Mary Ponjaley (?)

Smidt, Stough -- Jane Gordon, May 7, 1799

Shelton, Lewis -- Nancy Bonnell, Nov. 21, 1800

Timberlake, Samuel -- Mary Kitchens, Feb. 9, 1800

Tailer, Abraham -- Phoebe Williams, Sept. 3, 1799
(married May 2 ----

Whiting, Luke -- Barbara Patton, May 10, 1800

Williams, William -- Susan Paulding, Sept. 11, 1800

White, John H. -- Jane Surget, Nov. 13, 1800

Ankrett, John   -- Mary Galloway, 1805 (?)
Arnand, John P. -- Wilhemina Vortendorys, 27 March, 1806
Andrews, James   -- H.P. Girault, 26 June, 1810
Argo, Sanders   -- Sally Holland, 5 July, 1809
Anderson, George -- Margaret Kelly, Feb. 20, 1810
Anderson, Thomas -- Maria Nailer, 19 Sep. 1812
Aedry, Alexander -- Eliza Sutten, 21 May, 1814
Andrews, Philip -- Ann Rees, 10. Jan. 1815
Aswell, Hiram   -- Mary Saunders ------
Arnherst, John   -- Sara Houghton, 20 June, 1818
Alexander, Thomas -- M. McQuadde, 6 Aug. 1818
Anding, John   -- E. Freeman, 11 March, 1819

"B"

Bennett, Ezekiel -- Frances Cleveland, July, 1814
Brant, Joseph   -- Ribecca Bignal, 9 April, 1817
Barnard, William -- Barbara oster, 16 March, 1818
Breeden, John M. -- Louisa Beaumont, ------
Bowie, J.F.   -- Phebe Buford, 27 Sep. 1815
Benoist, Antonio -- Lessieux de La Croix, 21 Oct. 1809.
Bradley, James   -- Polly Ogilgby, 23 Dec. 1802
Burney, Samuel   -- Mary Allen, --1805
Benedict, Andy   -- Ann Terry, 9 July, 1805
Bonner, Willis   -- Jane Nailer, 25 Nov. 1807
Bond, Moses   -- Rosette Lacanture, 12 Dec. 1807
Bisland, Peter   -- Barbara Foster, 20 Dec. 1807
Balch, Hezikiah -- Maria West, 4 Jan. 1808
Belsinger, Henry -- Sarah Harman (f. Christian H-), 1.23.08
Brown, Elijah   -- Sara Kennison, 9 Feb. 1808
Bowie, J.F.   -- Polly Calvit, 16 Feb. 1808
Becker, Joseph   -- Betsy Brown, 2 Feb. 1808
Bell, James   -- Elizabeth Bosley, 15 April, 1808
Bedford, Isaac   -- Elizabeth Rowls, 14 May, 1808
Buford, Henry   -- Phebe Cochran, 10 June, 1808
Boland, Simeon   -- Helen Floyd, 23 June, 1808
Beaulieu, Joseph -- Elizabeth Annan 25 June, 1808
Brown, Samuel   -- Catherine Percy, 27 Sept. 1808
Bull, Joshua   -- Margaret Barton, 19 Nov. 1808
Brown, James   -- Rachel Dunn, 24 April, 1809
Bird, William   -- Elizabeth Lang, 9 May, 1809
Bedford, Isaac   -- Elizabeth Rowls, May 20, 1809
Baldwin, Levi   -- Rachel McCluskey, 12 June, 1809
Burns, David   -- Anna Ellen Ahjo, 24 Oct. 1809
Brown, Watson   -- Abigail Perkins, 31 March, 1810
Boland, Simeon   -- Lydia Cassells, 15 April, 1810
Barrett, Don Carlos -- Lucy Walton, 21 Jan. 1810
Benson, James   -- Anna Williams

Breeding, J. -- Violet Duncan, October 24, 1809
Briscoe, Parmenas -- Polly Montgomery. Dec.17, 1809
Bradshaw, William B. -- Mary Guice, Dec. 22, 1809
Brunner, Michael -- Mary Ormsby, (mother Mary Ormsby)
January 7, 1810
Benthruien, B.O. Van -- Polly Harrison, Feb. 24, 1810
Brabston, Thomas -- Anna Eldridge, Nov. 17, 1810
Boyd, John -- Elizabeth Miller, Dec. 20, 1810
Brown, Thomas -- Nancy Taylor, Jan.10, 1811
Bowman, Joseph -- Elizabeth Green -----
Bathos, John -- Mary Tyler, Jan. 30, 1812
Bower, Adams -- Eliza Moore, 20 April, 1812
Bullitt, William, Jr. -- Octavia O. Fannill, April 23,1812
Butler, Samuel -- Cynthia Brown, May 19, 1813
Butler, Thomas -- Ann Ellis, August 15, 1813.
Bradley, Archibald -- Phebe Swayze, --1813
Boon, Joseph -- Sally Tyler, 1813

"C"

Copeland, Jesse -- Polly Brown, ------
Cory, David -- Sarah Eastis (between 1802-1805)
Cochrane, George -- Tempa Hoster -- 1803
Carroll, John -- Dosey McCreey, 1807
Carter, Isaac -- Elizabeth Lambert, 1808
Corcy, David -- Patsy Harick (or Herrick)--- 1808
Calacote, James -- Patsy Middleton, ---1808
Custard, Morris -- Polly Boyd, -- --1808
Currie, Malsolm -- Rhoda Farrar, -- 1808
Crow, James -- Elener Garner, -- 1808
Curtis, Edward -- Nancy Clark, -- 1808
Carnahan, John -- Mercy Harrison, --1808
Crow, James -- Elener Garner, --1808
Cason, Robert -- Delia Adams - --1809
Coleman, R.F. -- Ann Pate --1809
Chandler, Josiah -- Polly Vernon, 1809
Calvit, William -- Elizabeth Spires, 1809
Coleman, Noah -- Patience Tanner, 1810
Claiborne, T.A. -- A.C.H. Wooldridge, 1809-1810
Crawford, William -- Nancy McCurry, 1810
Chany, George -- Sally Bartlett, --1810
Carabahal, Francis -- Elizabeth Morris ---
Camp, J. -- Elvira T. Bell -- 1811
Carr, Joseph -- Sarah Clifton -- 1812
Cleveland, Josiah M. -- Elexia L. Warren -- 1812
Campbell, Charles -- Selah Carter, --1813
Cason, Charles -- Mary Stoddard -- 1813
Collins, William -- Mary Foster -- 1814
Crow, Clark -- Peggy Yerby - 1814
Cortelle, Peter -- F. Hoggabt- 1814
Carson, Joseph -- C.C. I. Green - 1814
Camp, John -- Ann Fordham -----
Collins, W. -- Mary Foster- 1814
Calvit, Alexander -- Barbara Wood --1814

Cass, J.W. -- Ellen Herson, --1815
Cord, James -- Martha Hendon -- 1817
Carter, Isaac -- Joan Floyd, - 1817
Creighton, J. -- --- Anthony -- 1818

"D"

Dunbar, William -- Martha Willis -1803 or 1805
Davis, Sam -- Rhoda Standley, ---1805
Dewel, James -- Elizabeth Taylor --1805
Delaney, William -- Patsy Hannon, ---1808
Dorson, S.W. -- Elizabeth Conner- 1808
Dunbar, James -- Elizabeth Bisland- 1808
Dunbar, Joseph -- Olivia Magruder -- 1808
Leval, Elisha -- Behetalon Donnelly- 1810
Ducayet, J.M.B. -- Flora Ritier- 1810
Lrigass, Ephiram -- Elizabeth Weed - 1810
Daugharty, George -- Elizabeth Sojournore- 1810
David, John -- Rebecca Morris - between 1810-1812
Dana, John -- Catherine Walton --1811
Duncan, Stephen -- Margaret Ellis - 1811
Lodge, Jedediah -- Jane Goodcourage - 1811
Dixon, William -- Nancy Sanders - 1812
Dunbar, Isaac -- Mary Wilkinson- 1812
Day, Benjamin -- Lydia Martin -- 1813
Dyharron, William -- Marian Foster- 1814
Dews, Thomas -- Milly Blackwell -1818
Darrah, J. -- Ann Rieves - 1817
Dixon, William -- Janet Fowls -- 1817 -1818
Davis, John -- Elizabeth Alston -- 1818
Dubay, John -- Betsy Allen -- 1818
Lurr, Jacob -- Catherine Brown -- 1818
Davis, Gardner -- Annarette Balaner - 1818
Lriggs, Josiah -- Bathas M----
Degrash, William -- Anna Morgan

"E"
Eastes, William -- Nancy Walker -- 1805
England, William -- Rhoda Bullen -- 1808
Eaton, Thomas -- Sarah King -- 1808
Eldridge, Holland -- Elizabeth Armstrong - 1808
Eldridge, Thomas -- Catherine King
Elliott, Daniel D. -- Catherine Surget -1809
Edwards, Leonard -- Frances Longmire -- 1809
Erby, William -- Elsy Frisby --1810
Evans, William -- Sara Corail --1811
Ewing, Thomas -- --- Sewain - 1814
Eaten, Ephiram -- Elizabeth Cory -1816

"F"

Fanat, Jacob -- Catherine Hughes - 1805
Ford, George -- Penny Dunn (f. Richard Dunn) 30 Jan.1808
Fetty, Thomas - Betsy Whiting, 10 March, 1808
Ford, Abraham - Nellie Taylor, 15 April, 1808

Ford, B. -- Judith Perry -- 1808
Forgeth, John -- Mary Harman- 1808
Ferguson, Aaron -- Patsy Callahan -- 1809
Frotwell, R.B. -- Mary Gibson, --1810
Fox, William -- Ann Hatch -- 1810
Fleetwood, Whitney -- Mary Stevenson -1810
Fry, Jacob -- Catherine Myers --- 1811
French, Robert -- Nelly Hosey --1811
Flores, Joseph -- Margaret McCoy --1811
Fuller Oliver W. -- Marie Morrison, --1812
Ferguson, William -- Elizabeth Henderson, 1812-1813
Felter, John -- Stacy Floyd, -- 1813
Freeman, N. -- Julianna Sullivan, --1814
Fanah, Daniel -- Elizabeth King, -- 1814
Fry, Thomas -- Susannah Brown, --1814
Floyd, John -- Hannah White, -- 1814
Fuller, Benjamin -- Jane Perry, - 1817
Fagan, Robert -- Camilla Ratliff, -- 1817
Ford, Robert -- Nancy Harslip, -- 1818
Ferguson, Joseph -- Mary Freeman, -- 1819

"G"

Graham, Richard -- Mary Glasscock, --1805
Gilbert, Samuel -- Dicey Hughes -- 1805
Gince, Abraham -- Martha Cade -- 1805
Gaydon, G.L. -- Sally Evans --1808
Griffin, Thomas -- Nancy Hosea --1808
Grafton, Allen -- Elizabeth Wylie --1808
Grivet, William -- Eupha Robb - 1808
Gerice, Daniel -- Delia Williams----1808
German, Asa -- Elizabeth Barland, 1808
Gibson, John A. -- Polly Lain, 1809
Groom, Valentine -- Letetia Smith, 1809
Galbraith, Robert D. -- Mary Fabrean, 1811
Gray, Pierre -- Polly Adams, 1811
Ganey, John -- Pharaby Sutton, 1812
Grafton, Daniel -- Mary Flemming, 1812
Griffin, Isham -- Margaret Lord, 1813
Greenleaf, David -- Pamelia Gore, 1813
Griffin, Absalom -- Scythia Cale, 1814
Green, Charles B. -- Helen P. Adams, 1814
Gilleaspy, H. -- Jane Fletcher, 1814
Gray, James -- Harriett Smith, 1817
Gills, William -- Hannah Gardner, ------
George, William -- Mary Hoggatt, 1817
Gale, Thomas -- Margaret Green, 1818
Girault, F.S. -- Jane Kemper, 1818
Green, Richard -- Isabella Flemming, 1818
Gillespie, James A. -- Maria Smith, 1818
Goldman, -- Mary Fait, 1818
Gayden, Griffin. -- Dorcas Wade, 1818-1819
Girault, John R. -- Anna E. Moore ,-----
Grant, Travis -- Mary Brown, 1819

Holden, Simon -- Sarah Kennedy, May 9, 1805
Hardiman, J. -- Lucretia Nash, June 8, 1805
Hook, Simon -- Barbara James, Feb. 28, 1802
Harvard, Elijah -- Rachel Wells, March 13, 1803
Hobbs, Meredith -- Patsy Rule, December 19, 1805
Hulick, Abraham -- Elizabeth King, Dec. 19, 1806
Harding, Richard -- Charlotte Fortner, Jan. 12, 1808
Hogatt, Nathaniel -- Charlotte Smith, Jan. 14, 1808
Houston, Anthony -- Testimonials granted him as elder in
Methodist church, July, 1808.
Harrison, James -- Polly Edwards, April 17, 1808
Hoggatt, Wilford -- Elizabeth Merrell, Nov. 13, 1808
Hellum, Thomas - minister, authorized to solemnize mar-
riages, 2nd Monday in Jan., 1809
Hill, Phil -- Elizabeth Terry, May 22, 1809 (married
May 25, 1809)
Hoggatt, William -- Lucy Callahan, Sept. 12, 1809
Havard (Harvard), J. -- Joyce Howard (widow), Oct.8, 1809
Harrison, Joseph -- Nancy Nickols, Oct. 9, 1809
Howell, Eben -- Elizabeth Swayze, Nov.11, 1809
Hunter, Pleasant -- Martha Ketchner, Dec. 26, 1809
Higdon, William- Testimonials- Elder in Methodist Church
- April 14, 1809
Hutchins, John -- Betsy Towson, March 31, 1810
Harper, Miles - Testimonials- Elder in Methodist Church,
2nd Monday in October, 1810.
Howard, Joshua -- Drusilla Rogers, May 17, 1811
Harrison, James G. -- Elizabeth Morris, July 12, 1811
Hunter, John -- Mary Ellison, Nov. 4, 1811
Hoggatt, Nathaniel -- Jane Barney, Nov. 11, 1811
Harrigill, John -- Cynthia Gibson, Dec. 20, 1811
Hewsberger, Jacob -- Susan McHenry, Dec. 20, 1811
Holmes, John P. -- Freelove Ford, Jan. 6, 1812
Hall, Isaac -- Nancy Wythe, Feb. 25, 1812
Hopkins, J.A. -- Eugenia Darrache, April 7, 1812
Hendon, Josiah -- Patsy Pruett, August 8, 1812
House, John -- Drucilla Douglas, April 25, 1814
  "   "   " married 28 April, 1814,
by Edwin Andrews, J. P.
Heddy, Elijah -- Mary Webb, August 16, 1814
Hinton, Thomas -- Mary Andrews (widow), Nov. 18, 1815
Haslett, Andrew -- Ann ... Conners, Feb. 2, 1817
Howard, Thomas -- Lucy Mock, March 6, 1817
Huntington; Henry W. -- Helen Dunbar,
Hinds, B.M. -- Ruth Newman, May 18, 1817
Hail, Nicholas -- Charlotte Evans, May 19, 1818
Hannon, Thomas-- Dorcas Hamilton, April 5, 1818
Hoggatt, John. -- Jane Melton, May 21, 1818
Hosea, Brannison -- Nancy Howett, --15, 1818
Harper, Wilson -- Tapany Barland, March 6, 1818
Horn, John F. -- Margaret Rickey, April 1, 1819
Hunter, Henry -- Helen Drake, April 25, 1817
Henderson, Charles -- Dicy Bass, 1812
Holmes, Robert -- Rebecca (?) Swayse, Jan. 8, 1814

Hamson, Jonathan, -- Anna Williams, 1814
Hooten, Lewis -- Sarah Acres, 1814

"I"

Irwin, Walter -- Mary Johnson, August 10, 1805
Inge, Haley -- Elizabeth W. Cox, March 17, 1809
Irby, William -- Elsey Frisby -----

"J"

Jonas, John -- Catherine Miller, May 25, 1803
Johnson, Jordan -- Sarah Burney, 1808
Johnson, John -- Susan Cook, Sept. 7, 1808
Jett, Martin -- Tabitha Kirkland, 1810
Jenkins, Josiah -- Rachel Herrington, 1813
Jones, Wilec -- ----- Sidell, April 25, 1814
Jones, J.C. -- Maria Violency, Feb. 26, 1818
Jones, Charles -- Esther Holbrook, May 23, 1818
Johnson, James -- Susan Lape, May 23, 1818
Jordan, John -- Sarah Conner, 5 May, 1819
Jerome, James -- Margaret Stewart, June 6, 1815

"K"

Killian, David -- Nancy Hughes, March 14, 1802
Kirkland, William -- Betsy Newcome, May 29, 1802
Kell, Thomas -- Patsy Thompson, March 5, 1808
King, John -- Dolly Daughtery, Sept. 20, 1809
Knight, George -- Charity Hamilton, Oct. 11, 1809
King, Elisha -- Lida McCoy, March 26, 1810
Kirkham, James -- Rachel Rollins, July 2, 1811
King, Samuel -- Eliza Gilbert, April 5, 1813
Kerchivan, James -- Susan T. Beckett (widow), March 23,
1813
Haylip, William -- Nancy Overacker, March 24, 1814
Kirkham, Spencer -- .S. Neeland, April 16, 1814
Knox, Samuel -- Mary Scotthorn, March 16, 1818
Keen, Thomas -- Elizabeth Gibson, June 16, 1818
King, Edward P. -- Levicy Morris, August 1, 1818

"L"

Lloyd, Elijah -- Nancy Dyer, Jan. 20, 1803
Lusk, Jack -- Rebecca Lloyd, Dec.10, 1807
Leizeger, Joseph -- Susan Neff, May 28, 1808
Little, Peter -- Elizabeth Law, April 15, 1808
LeCompte, James -- Silva Brosse, June 24, 1808
Lusk, John -- Elizabeth Cassell, July 30, 1808
Lattimore, William -- Cecelia Lee, Feb. 25, 1809
Leake, William -- Rachel Selser, April 5, 1809
Lang, John -- J. Wilson, August 5, 1809
Langdon, Richard C. -- Letitia Hancock, August 17, 1810
Liddell, Joseph -- Sarah Hill, Jan. 17, 1811
Lusk, Eli -- Margaret McNamee, March 5, 1811

Leek, Frederick   -- Mary Robb, Sept. 26, 1814
Lusk, Thomas   -- **Mary Green**, March 2, 1813
Lazarus, Thomas   -- Betsy Murray, ---
Lewis, Joel   -- Rebecca Porter, Jan. 16, 1812
Luyster, Garrett   -- Mary Campbell, **Jan.** 3, 1817
Lyon, Joseph -- Auroa Cox, April 23, 1808
Long, James   -- Jane H. Wilkinson, May 13, 1815

"M"

McCarty, Amos   --   Ruth Elmore (mo. Ruth Elmore), March 17
1813
Miller, Alexander   -- Polly McCurdy, 18 May, 1813
Mahan, Arthur -- Catherine Jenkins, July 5, 1813
Montgomery, Hugh   -- Jane Montgomery (f. William Mont-
gomery), Nov. 20, 1813
McComos, H.   -- Nancy Willis, (mo. Sara Chotard), Jan.5'14
Madden, Emanuel   -- Charity Carroll, Aug. 3, 1814
McGill, James -- Penelope Coleman, Aug. 15, 1814
Mace, Richard   -- Margaret McHenry, June 30, 1817
Morris, Benjamin -- Elizabeth D----, Jan. 23, 1818
Michie, David -- Isabella Cochrane, Dec. 17, 1805
Miller, Thomas G.   -- Parthena Rowan, March 25, 1818
McCarroll, Charles   -- etsy Higdon, 1809
McGlanghlin -----   ---- Kennon (f. William), March 9,'05
May, Stone   -- Patsy Fuqua (f. Joseph Fuqua), April 11'05
Morgan, D.B.   -- Eliza B. Middleton(f. Elisha Middleton),
May 23, 1805
Manning, Joseph   -- Elizabeth Aswell, July 1, 1805
Miller, Abel -- Nancy Perkins, July 6, 1805
Miller, John   -- Mary Kennison, March 25, 1806
Mulkey, Ellis -- Mary Floyd, Dec. 14, 1807
McAllister, Charles   -- Catherine Black, Feb. 17, 1808
Martin, James   -- N.B. Miller, Oct. 20, 1808
McCarson, Samuel   -- Julianna Dennison, 1808
McAtee, Thomas   --   Mary McIntyre, Oct. 22, 1808
McClure, Rev. John   Elder in Methodist Church, Jan. 1808
McCarroll, Charles   -- Betsy Higdon, March 9, 1809
Moore, L.H.   -- Ann Childress, April 6, 1809
Mitchell, P.P.   -- Eliza Burney (consent of Joseph
Burney), May 3, 1809
Morgan, John   -- Patsy Blunt, August 18, 1809
McConnell, James -- Julia Forgett, August, 1809
Marten, Enoch   -- Elizabeth Hilderbrand, Sept. 4, 1809
McCaleb, Samuel   -- Sarah Smith, Sept. 9, 1809
McQuiddy, Thomas   --Mary Armstrong, Oct. 11, 1809
Moore, Samuel   -- Ann Boyd, 2 Nov. 1809
Moore, L.H.   -- Ann Childress, April 9, 1809
Morford, William   -- Nancy Smith, Sept. 8, 1810
McNamee, John -- Anna Price, Sept. 30, 1810
McCaroll, Charles   -- Betsy Higdon, 1809
McConnell, James   -- Julianna Forgett, 1810
May, Martin,   --   Sally Bannoser, March 31, 1810
McKhany, Charles   -- Susan Reach, May 15, 1810

McMillan, --- -- Sally Foster, June 27, 1810
Miles, Osburne -- Elizabeth Barr, Dec. 25, 1810
McKenzie, Andrew -- Louisa Calvit, Jan. 31, 1811
Morford, William -- Nancy Smith (widow), 1811
Moore, James -- Maria Yarbough, May 30, 1811
Marshall, Thomas W. -- Delby Mion, Jan. 12, 1809
McNiece, Abraham -- Susan Miller, April 24, 1811
Montgomery, John -- Ann Cochrane, Oct. 15, 1811
McYerke, Charles -- Hannah Hogan, Dec. 25, 1811
Martin, John -- Elizabeth Erwin, July 22, 1812
Malone, Vincent -- Sarah Scriggs, 1812

"N"

Nerson, Isaac -- Ellen Foster (between years 1803-1805)
Newcommer, John -- Pierry Kembal, 1808
Nolly, Richard -- Thomensey Connelly, 1809
Newman, George -- Charlotte Dunbar, 1809
Nouchet, A.B.Z. -- C.A. De Lacroix, 1809
Newelle, George -- Lydia Howard, 1810
Nevitt, John B. -- Mary Shilling, 1810
Neill, James -- Abigail Kemball, 1811
Newton, Elias -- Elizabeth Powell, 1811
Norton, Charles -- Mary Terrell, 1812
New, David -- Polly Shepherd, 1813
Nicholls, Nathaniel -- Isabella Nuchie (?), 1813
Noyes, Henry -- Mary Ellis, 1813
Nelson, Peter -- M. Hollands, 1813
Nevitt, John B. -- Sarah Banks, 1818
Neito, Joseph -- Mary Ann Gomas, 1818
Newton, Elias -- Margaret Neighbours, 1815

"O"

Odain, Moses -- Louisa Gibson, 1808
Ogslesby, Sabret -- Betsy Wilson, 1810
Overton, W.H. -- Harriett Winters, 1811
O'Neill, James -- Eleanor Brunell, 1813
Owens, Alexander -- Polly Rose, 1813
O'Dom, Moses -- Sabra Chambers, 1819

"P"

Postlewaite, Samuel -- Ann Dunbar, 1805
Parkinson, Robert -- Mary Boardman, 1805
Perkins, Ezekiel -- Elizabeth Hamon, 1805
Perry, John L. -- Mary Fenton, 1808
Porter, John -- Mary Middleton, 1808
Pennington, William -- Sarah Faurer. 1808
Prather, Stephen -- Elizabeth Ploesdon, 1809
Parkin, George -- Rosanna Ross, 1809
Pomet, Vincent -- Margaret Anxtive (?), 1809
Powell, Thomas -- Mary Green, 1809
Pipes, Joseph -- Jane Grisham, 1810

Pipes, Abraham   --   Elizabeth Grisham, 1810
Parker William   --   Abigail Armstrong, 1810
Purviance, Robert   --   Elizabeth McLaine, 1810
Plowden, Bannister   --   Catherine Price, 1810
Plowden, Eliphalet   --   Margaret Williams, 1811
Potter, Caleb   --   Priscilla Myers, 1811
Page, John   --   Elizabeth Holmes, 1811-1812
Pennell(?), John M.   --   Kinmah Yarbough, 1811
Pease, Gamamiel   --   Catherine Brunner, 1811
Patterson, Samuel   --   Polly Forgatt, 1811
Powell, William   --   Betsy Griggan, 1811
Phelps, Thomas F.   --   Sarah Stephenson, 1812
Poultner (Poultney ?), James   --   Catherine Vincent, 1812
Pipes, Thomas   --   Winifred Huey, April, 1812
Parkins, George   --   Ann Anderson, 1812- 1813
Price, Simon   --   Martha Smith, 1813
Pipes, Abner   --   Nancy Terrell, 1813
Parker, John   --   Rebecca McLaughlin ---
Parnall, Levi   --   Mary Van, 1813
Perkins, Isaac   --   Evney Bullin, 1814
Parker, John   -- Rebecca McLaughlin --
Pipes, Abner   --   Nancy Fenall, 1814
Phipps, John   --   Martha McClelland
Perkins, Charles   --   Elizabeth Harrison Feb.8, 1819
Pierson, Henry   --   Susan Vaughn, April 8, 1819
Pomet, Leonard   --   Francoise Coce -----

"R"

Ragan, Thomas --   Hannah Stilton, Sept. 27, 1803
Rossett, Francis   --   Mary Rose Portiers, Jan. 19, 1808
Richie, Thomas H.   --   Sarah Read, March 20, 1808
Row, William   --   Rebecca Wimbish, Nov. 9, 1808
Roberts, Daniel   --   Sarah Griffin, March 6, 1809
Richow, Jacob   -- ministers bond·
Rulon, Ephiram   --   Helen Hasencliver, Feb. 20, 1807
Roach, Richard   --   Elizabeth Collins, Jan. 18, 1810
Rose, Enoch   --   Margaret Wade, March 16, 1810
Ripley, Samuel   --   Mary Donally, Jan. 14, 1812
Roach, Benjamin   --   Elizabeth Greenfield, Feb. 23, 1811
Roundtree, Elisha   --   Charlotte McQuirton, Jan. 2, 1812
Richardson, Samuel   --   Elisa McWilliams, April 15, 1812
Richardson, Moses   --   J.E.N. Brown, March 5, 1813
Rossett, Francois   --   Killena Williams, March 5, 1813
Rose, Philip   --   Patsy Hogg, August 13, 1813
Rabb, William   --   Elizabeth Duell, March 17, 1814
Regan, Malichi   --   Rachel Jenkins, 1814
Risley, Oliver   --   Susanna Arbour, Oct. 11, 1814
Roundtree, William   --   Elizabeth Hays, 30 March, 1818
Rice, George   -- Barbary Brown, July 11, 1805
Rummell, Christian   -- Hannah Hoarkins 1808
Read, Clement N.   --   D. E. Whittington, 1808
Reed, Abner   --   Margaret Tooley, 1808
Routh, John   --   Ann Smith ---

Simmonds, Edward   --   Rachel Terry, 1805
Smith, Eli C   --   Mary Rule, 1805
Stout, William   --   Nancy Pungeor, 1803-1805
Swayze Elijah   --   Harriet Cory, 1807
Still, Elijah   --   Sarah Heady, 1808
Singleton, William   --   Sally Lunk (or Lank), 1808
Shilling, Mathew   --   Martha Middleton, 1808
Sturdivant --   - Sarah Perry, 1808
Smith, E.T.   --   Susannah Poole, 1809
Scott, Berryman   --   Naomi Porter, 1809
Smith, Edward T.   --   Susanna Pool, 1809
Strong, David   --   Susannah Briant, 1809
Shackney, David   --   Eliza Bradley, 1810
Shipp, William   --   Lucy Barnard, 1810
Seville, Joseph T.   --   Sarah Hill, 1810
Sanders, James   --   Maria Miller
Sossa, Joseph   --   Acegates Garcia, 1810
Schurlock, John   --   Jenny Aswell, 1810-1811
Swayse, Samuel P.   --   Maria Bradshaw, 1811
Selser, Isaac N.   --   Betsy Montgomery
Sleighter, Arthur   --   Mary Bell, 1812
Stone, Chris.   --   Ayrinthe E. Graham, 1812
Stevens, John   --   Mary Cole, 1813
Salisbury, N.B.   --   Elisha (?) Scruggs
Sarson, Andre Francois   --   Annie L----, 1813
Scurlock, J.   --   H.H. Swayze, 1814
Sugett, Francis   --   Eliza Dunbar, 1814
Snodgrass, John   --   Lydia Montgomery, 1814
Snoylie, James   --   Sarah Bisland, 1815
Semple, Joseph   --   Elizabeth Henderson, 1817
Scrivner, Levi   --   Jane Salters, 1817
Swayze, Nathan   --   Ann Waters, 1817
Sylvester, Joseph   --   Sarah Clapp, 1817
Still, T.J.   --   Jeminy Delancy, ---

"T"

Tarnhill, George   --   Rachel Foster, 1802
Taylor, John Todd   --   Cath rine Banker, 1802
Terry, Lewis   --   Nancy Crouch, 1802
Torress, Joseph   --   Sally Roes, 1803
Tardi, Matien   --   Leonora Laggaente, 1803
Towson, Ezekiel   --   Betsy Brooks Towson
Turner, William   --   Anna Sterrett, 1808
Thompson, Martin   --   Betsy Barland, 1809
Truax, James   --   Sally Floyd, 1809
Taylor, George W.   --   Jane Livingston, 1810
Tichner, Gabriel   --   Elizabeth Wallace, 1810
Townsend, George   --   Catherine Brown, 1811
Tuller, John   --   Mary Mitchell, 1811
Thruston, Edward T.   --   Sally Terrell
Turner, Edward   --   Elizabeth Baker, 1812-13
Tucker, Pennington   --   Susan Wade
Turpin, White   --   Rebecca Mc----, 1813
Thompson, Jonathan   --   Anna Williams, 1814

Thomas, Matthew -- Mary M. Cooper, 1814
Thompson , Hugh -- Sarah Lazarus, 1814
Thompson, R. -- Elizabeth Wisgart, 1814
Tooley, Henry -- Mary Droomggol, 1814
Tichlee, Christian -- Polly Gladwin, 1817
Tiernan, Peter -- Lydia Young, 1817
Tooley, Henry -- Susan Bledsoe, 1818
Tucker, Samuel -- Anne Llambo, 1818
Thompson, Richard -- Margaret ------
Thornberry, William -- Susan Ellis
Tribble John M. -- Elizabeth Cason, 1818 -1819
Tallady, Isaac -- Polly Long, 1819
Turner, Fielding -- Caroline Sargent, 1818

"W"

Waller, Joseph -- Polly Dowdles, May 10, 1810
Wilds, Davis J. -- S.W. Chaney, May 11, 1805
Wood, John -- Elizabeth Hogatt, May 17, 1805
Wonnell, J. -- Letty (?) Anderson, July 4, 1802
Wallace, James -- Margaret Wilson, Jun 19, 1803
Wells, John -- Sarah McChaney, May 15, 1805
Williams, William -- Eliza Ogden, Jan. 9, 1809
Waltman, I. -- Elizabeth Hambleton, April 13, 1809
Winn, J.W. -- M.L. Floyd, April 27, 1809
Wood, Thomas -- Mary Craven, April 21, 1809
Wentworth, Stephen -- Nancy Dorsey, August 12, 1809
Whitaker, Isaac -- Elizabeth Bullin, Jan.1, 1809
Wright, William -- Mary N. Hoggatt, May 18, 1810
Wilkins, James C. -- Charlotte Bingman, May 26, 1810
Wilkinson, William -- Elinor Foster (parents, James and
Elizabeth Foster),July 4, 1810
Williams, Thomas -- Sally Bodkins, Kan. 12, 1812
Wilkinson, Wyatt -- Eliza Griffin, Jan. 6, 1813
Weeks, Levi -- Ann Greenleaf, Jan. 9, 1813
Wilkinson, George F. -- Elvisa Freeland, Feb. 16, 1813
Williams, A.P. -- Elizabeth Routh, April 22, 1813
Wells, Samuel -- Frances Foster, Dec. 5, 1814
Ware, A.N. -- Sarah Ellis, October 1,1814
Wood, John B. -- Eliza Allen, June 5, 1817 (mo. Eliz.A.)
Wren, Thomas -- Melinda Ross, July 12, 1818
Whitehead --- - Polly Perry, July 16, 1818
Walker, William T. -- Martha Ratcliff, July 16, 1818
Walton, Parke -- Mary Winn, Dec. 17, 1818
Wyche, Henry -- Eliza Allison, Jan. 20, 1818
Wilson, Benjamin -- Nancy Philips, Jan. 3, 1818
Wood, Henry C. -- Marinah Walker, March 18, 1819

ADAMS COUNTY

MARRIAGES

1819 - 1823

Aldridge, Sylvester   -- Anna Ritha Ballance
Allen, William V.   -- Harriet Wilkins
Atkinson, Richard S.   -- Catherine Fry
Arnhearst, John   -- Susan Swayze
Andrews, Samuel   -- Matilda Sorrels
Augustus, John   -- Henrietta Shake
Aswell, Hinson   -- Caroline Johnson

"B"

Brazell, Drury W.   -- Mary Louise Barre
Barland, David   -- Susannah Pierson
Bower, Adam   -- Elizabeth French
Beach, Clark   -- Esther Hamilton
Bruce, William   -- Sarah Goodin
Breill, Setrick   -- Amelia Cipin
Brannan, Joseph   -- Elizabeth Taylor
Brown, Abram   -- Jane Server
Bennett, James   -- Mary Swaine
Bruntie, Louis Benjamin   -- Sophie Jouan (or Iouan)
Bell, H. Egbert   -- Anna F. Conner
Brown, Charles   -- Peggy Silkrage
Brown, Arthur   -- Maria Meast (or Weast)
Bradley, Robert   -- Mary Defrance
Braxton, William   -- Mary Watkins
Bradley, Bradford   -- Nancy Griffin
Bradshaw, James   -- Elizabeth Martin
Brill, Ernst   --- Catherine Brile
Bridges, Sampson   -- Maryann Foster
Braswell, Hardy G.   -- Lsabella McMillian
Beall, I. Hervey   -- Eliza Hopkins
Baker Peter P.   -- Harriet Conner
Billingham, Thomas B.   -- Mary Hall
Brittington, Purnel   -- Caroline Bradshaw

"C"

Chotard, Henry   ---Frances Minor
Cuzzens, John   -- Parthena Judkins
Catling, James   -- Susan Fleming
Cazarie, Paul G.   -- Anne C. Quegles
Cowdon, James   -- Sarah Ker
Carter, James L.   -- Mary Ann Prentice
Carter, Pharoah   -- Susan Griffin
Cipsna, S.W.H.   -- H. Maria Fuller
Carl, James   -- Elizabeth Seymore
Carmichael, Richard A.   -- Maria A. Green

Cason, Jese	-- Elizabeth Lucas
Cotton, Samuel	-- Jane E.N. Richardson
Conner, John	-- Rachel Williams
Cross (or Crops), Barney	-- Sally Miller

"D"

Dunban, Stephen	-- Catharine A. Bingaman
Dicks, John	-- Mary Farar
Dorsey, Silas	-- Elizabeth Wilkinson
Dunn, James L.	-- Mary Tucker
Davis, James G.	-- Elizabeth Ballance

"E"

Elsy, Abraham	-- Polly Spencer
Ely, Charles F.	-- Hetty Chaillie

"F"

Fields, Demsy	-- Susannah Williams
Freeland, Thomas	-- Sarah Skinner
Frazer, John	-- Elizabeth Mardis
Foster, Job	-- Isabella Campbell
Fields, Robert	-- Charlotte Brooks

"G"

Gardner, Thompson	-- Sarah Glenn
Grayson, John T.	-- Sarak Covington
Gordon, Edward	-- Catherine Bradshaw
Glover, John	-- Agnes Larkin
Griffith, Elias B.	-- Ann E.C. Brooks
Gardner, James	-- Mary Baillie
Gordon, James	-- Susan Fields
Galtney, Joseph	-- Charlotte Hazlip
Griffin, David	-- Elizabeth Sipsions (or Sessions)

"H"

Holmes, Robert	-- Sally Davis
Howard, Joshua, Jr.	-- Mariah Dodd
Hoeter, Jacob	-- Hannah Rumley
Hosea, John	-- Nancy Woods
Hough, Lewis H.	-- Sarah Hardesty
Hulburd, Hiland	-- Maria Mitchell
Hall, John E.	-- Catherine Million
Hazzard, William	-- Charlotte Leaper
Hason, Edward	-- Rebecca Roberts
Hall, Joseph	-- Elizabeth Cason
Holmes, Simpson	-- Julia Ann Dodd
Henderson, George	-- Jane Row

"J"

Jones, William	- - Eliza Kiernan
Jones, John	-- Rebecca Price
Johnson, Hiram	-- Elizabeth Turner

"K"

Kay, Gabriel	-- Anne D. Andrews
Ker, John	-- Mary Baker
King, Jacob	-- Jane Eliza Gormley
Kidd, Edward	-- Polly Dougherty

"L"

Lattimore, David	-- Emily Wilkins
Lum, Samuel	-- Ann Owings
Luse, Nathan R.	-- Nancy Swayze
Lemos, Domingo	-- Julian Ceravaxal
Lum, Eratus	-- Sanai A. Foster
Lum, Lewis	-- Cynthe Harrison
Lane, Orlando	-- Isabella Nichols
Lowery, David	-- Catherine Rouk
Lapice, P.M.	-- Mary Louise Demie
Lewis, Francis	-- Lucinda Montgomery
Lemon, William	-- Judith Lindsay

"M"

Murry, Hosea	-- Sarah Tooley
May, Richard H.	-- Elizabeth Davis
McLendon, John L.	-- Lavina Glassburn
Mardis, Abner	-- Ebeline Tier
Moore, James	-- Eliza Ford
Miller, James	-- Adelia Johnston
Magruder, John H.	-- Margaret Skinner
McCoffey, Hugh	-- Sarah Neyland
Moss, Howell	-- Rebecca H. Ross
Moss, Nashville	-- Charlotte W. Brooks
McCamant, Samuel	-- Margaret Tyler
McAllister, Charles	-- Sarah Blue
McDonald, John	-- Susan Wilson
Marler, Samuel J.	-- Lovisy T. Davis
Montgomery, Samuel, Jr.	-- Rebecca Alexander
Morgan, Thomas	-- Mary Armstrut
Montgomery, John	-- Sarah Brown
Moss, Henry	-- Balinda Snodgrass
Moore, David	-- Eliza Truman
Martin, K. David	-- Rebecca Swayze
Moore, John	-- Rachel Bacon
Miles, David	-- Ellen Brown
McVay, Joseph	-- Mary Killion

"N"

Norman, Elijah   -- Elizabeth Swain
Nelson, Marson   -- Mary Hoover
Noyes, William T.   -- Mary Miles Boyce
Nixon, Thomas   -- Margarett Hankinson
Nugent, John   --- Amelia G. Forman
Norton, F. William   -- Matilda Bruster

"O"

Outer, Jacob   -- Hannah Rumley

"P"

Pigmal, Francis   -- Amelaiede Noschette
Parker, Walter S.   -- Elizabeth H. Graham
Pomet, Joseph, Jr.   -- Cloe Tear
Pollard, George   -- Lauren Tier
Pratt, Willoughby L.   -- Eliza Bickle
Peters, John   -- Sarah Blain
Perry, Samuel   -- Elizabeth Downs
Piggott, Robert   -- Eliza A. Perkins
Pettibone, Chauncey   -- Susan Brandon
Patterson, John   -- Catherine Bisland
Purnell, John M.   -- Rebecca Howell

"R"

Reeves, John   -- Nelly Chambers
Robetaille, Louis   -- Mariah Burtis
Rowan, Thomas   -- Sarah O. Wright
Reed, Darius   -- Caroline Roach
Rabourn, David   -- Catherine Bradshaw
Robb, William   -- Sarah Turner
Read, James T.   --- Ann Croxan
Ringrose, William   -- Polly Swain
Rabb, A.W   -- Mary Jane Fletcher

"S"

Stanard, Hugh   -- Ann Simpson
Sourwalt, Frederic   -- Catherine Tetrican
Southworth, Peter   -- Elizabeth Fisher
Scott, William   -- Margaret Duffin
Sharp, Absalom   -- Clarissa Thomas
Salisbury, John R.   -- Eliza Hoggatt
Swing, James   -- Ann Voris
Sanderson, John A.   -- Louisiana Montgomery
Sepious, Boon   -- Jane Hoggatt
Smith, R. William   -- Anna Henderson
Swayze, Jacob   -- Cynthia Ford
Spires, Jesse G.W.   -- Maacha Killion

"T"

Tooley, Henry	-- Elizabeth Davis
Tucker, Joseph	-- Hannah Huston
Terrell, Richard	-- Sucretia (Lucretia?) Martin
Turner, Robert, Jr.	-- Frances Foster
Thomas, Charles E.	-- Caroline Sandoze
Timmons, Joseph	-- Margaret Powell
Taylor, William	-- Elizabeth Owens
Thornsburgh, John	--: Mary Ralph
Taylor, Joseph	-- Elizabeth Brownjohn

"V"

Van, Allin	-- Harriett Wilkins
Vidal, Louis A.	-- Lucinda Rutherford

"W"

Woods, Samuel	-- Joanna T. Demsy
Wood, David	-- Eliza C. Bowman
Wheeler, Warren	-- Elenor Bailey
Wilson, James	-- Polly McCarley
Wells, Noell	-- Sarah Frisby
Whitehurst, John	-- Elizabeth Cobler
Warren, Seth W.	-- Sinah Glasscock
Wade, William	-- Mary Owens
Wailes, Benjamin L.S.	-- Rebecca S.M. Covington
Winston, Lewis	-- Mary Wright
Woods, James	-- Lucinda Hopkins
Way, James	-- Elizabeth Caraxal
Wade, Nathaniel C.	-- Elizabeth Wilkshire
Wortell, Abram	-- Sarah Jones
Wood, John	-- Clarissa Cole
Walker, William T.	-- Marie Weigart
Webster, John	-- Mimy Gregory
Wade, Benjamin	-- Zeli Robetaille
Williams, Daniel	-- Mary Lamb
Waag, Carlass	-- Wiellemiene Fienkee

" Y "

Young, Jesse P.	-- Elizabeth Webb
Yates, Levi	-- Sarah Stewart

"Z"

Zegler, Richard	-- Elizabeth Tucker

TYCER, RICHARD WILLIAM.

August 16, 1811.
Wife: Jannet. Legatees: Jannett Tycer (wife), Thos.
Tycer (brother), a negro slave named "Adam" to have
freedom. Admrs: wife, John Lowry and James McKnight.
Wit: Mary Neilson, John Brown and Joseph Lowry.

DAVIS, JOHN.

October 24, 1810.
Daughters: Addy, Lucy, Olevia, Jency, Polly and Rosanna.
Son: Davis. Administratrix: wife Mary Davis.
Wit: Benjamin Harvey, Nathan Chamberlin and Abner Green.

BURRIS, SAMUEL.

Probated June 18, 1812.
Son: John and other children.
Administratrix: wife Mary.   Wit: John Wilson, Craddock
Gober.

FUTCH, JACOB B.

March 31, 1812. October 19, 1812.
Wife: Prucilla. Son: Redding. Admr: Hardy Coward.
Wit: Abraham Truel and William Brown.

DRENNAN, DAVID.

June 1, 1811.
Daughters: Martha, Elizabeth, Alice, Sarah. Son: William.
Admrs: wife Ruth Drennan and son William Drennan.
Wit: Thomas Waggoner, Polly Waggoner and Robert Griffin.

MEREDITH, THOMAS.

September 15, 1808.
Sons: John, Thomas and James. Daughters: Mary, Cathren
and Sarah. Wife: Abigail. Admrs: none.
Wit: John Graham, Eli Elkins and Reuben Hollis.

LOWRY, ROBERT.

October 9, 1813.
Wife: Penelope. Daughters: Elizabeth, Jane, **Mary** Ann.
Sons: John Robert and Joseph Lowry. Admrs: three sons.
Wit: James McKnight and Benjamin Cassels.

CURRY, JACOB.

Nov. 18, 1813. April 21, 1814.
Wife: Avis Curry. Daughters: Lucy, Elizabeth and Mary.
Admrs: wife, George Ellis, Thomas Bickham (friends).
Wit: Robert Griffin, Holloway Huff and Hackley Warren.

LANE, THOMAS.

April 5, 1814. October 17, 1814.
Legatees: Thomas Moore (nephew) and Sarah Bryant (niece).
Admrs: Samuel Moore, Henry Anderson and Robert Thornhill.
Wit: Henry Swearingen, Littleton Seal and Eli Mercer.

CAIN, HARDY.

July 1, 1814. October 14, 1814.
Wife: Mary Cain. Daughter: Mary. Sons: William, James
and Isaiah Cain. Admrs: wife and son James.
Wit: Angus Wilkinson, Isaiah Cain and William Cain.

KNOX, ARCHIBALD.

October 19, 1815.
Wife: Martha Knox. Daughters: Elizabeth, Martha, Anna,
Sarah and Rebecca. Son: Samuel. Admrs: wife, Alexander
Jackson and Hugh Cooper (sons-in-law).
Wit: John Cain, Angus Wilkinson and William Cain.

COTTEN, THOMAS.

February 19, 1816.
Wife: Anne. Daughters: Nancy, Susanna and Elizabeth.
Sons: Sam, John, Abel, Asa and Thomas.
Admrs: wife, Thomas Cotten and Willis Cotten (sons).
Wit: Thomas Torrence, Jesse Rice and Joseph Robertson.

(There are two Will Books in Amite County marked # 1.
The first being the book used when Mississippi was known
as Territory of Mississippi and the second Will Book marked as Will Book #1, was used after the State was admitted
to the Union.)

GAYDEN, GEORGE.

May 29, 1819. June 8, 1819.
Daughters: Rebecca Batchelor, Patsey Perkins, Elizabeth
Morgan, Diana Davis, Hannah Gayden (dau.-in-law), Gere-
fina Gayden (gr.dau.).
Sons: Cadesbey Gayden, Agrippa Gayden, George L. Gayden,
Griffin Gayden, and grandsons, Francis and George Gayden
Wren. Exrs: sons Cadesbey, Agrippa and George L.
Wit: Daniel Wilkinson, William Morgan.

WREN, JOHN.

May 18, 1818. December Term of Court, 1818.
Legatees: Rebecca Caroline Lowry, Harriet Matilda Lowry and "the Administrator is to maintain a certain
child in Liberty, said to be the offspring of me."
Admr: Robert L. Lowry. Wit: G.Gayden.

CALLIHAN, PATRICK.

November 7, 1817. September 7, 1818.
Wife: Catharine Callihan. Sons: Richard, David, George
Washington, Robert McFarlane Callihan. Daughter: Elizabeth
Callihan. Exrs: wife, David Lea and Thomas Torrance.
Wit: R. Hurst and Caleb Benton.

WHITE, MARY.

September 24, 1817. September 6, 1819.
Sons: James, David, Alfred White. "Harry is to be taken
care of by the family" (relationship not given).
Daughters: Sarah White, Effy Dear, Elizabeth Kennon.
Exrs: sons James White and David White, John W. Kennon.
Wit: David Winborne and Josse McKay.

KING, WILLIAM.

September 16, 1819. October 25, 1819.
Legatees: Davis King (brother) and William King (nephew).
Exrs: John Burton and Gabriel Felder (friends).
Wit: Charles Davis, James Hinson and Edmond Jenkins.

CARTER, CHARLES.

August 2, 1819. October 25, 1819.
Legatees: wife Mary Carter and children, Sarah Martin,
James F. Thomas and John M. Exrs: Archibald McGeehee
and Caleb Higginbottom (friends).
Wit: W. Mansfield, Hugh B. Johnson , Lawson Higginbottom.

RAMBERT, JOHN.

Nov. 15, 1819. Dec. 5, 1819.
Legatees: James, Zackous, John, Andrew, Judy and Charlotte
(children by a former marriage), children by last marriage
mentioned, but not named. Exr: William Libby McKoy.
Wit: Middleton Kneeland, Jesse McKay and Charles McKay.

WITHERSPOON, JAMES E.

July 25, 1820. September 5, 1820.
Legatees: wife Elizabeth and Thomas McFadden Witherspoon
(brother).   Exrs: wife and Charles Story Witherspoon (brother-in-law). Wit: Robert Witherspoon, Robert P. Witherspoon and Mary Witherspoon.

WITHERSPOON, JAMES.

June 11, 1820. October 30, 1820.
Wife: Hester Witherspoon. Daughters: Hester Jane Capels,
Mary Story Burrows, Ann Reese Knox, Elizabeth Witherspoon,
Lenora Witherspoon. Sons: James Alexander, John Gardner,
Charles Story and Edwin Reese Witherspoon.
Exrs: James A., John G., Charles S. and Edwin R. Wither-
spoon (sons) and Thomas Torrance (friend).
Wit: R. Hurst, Archibald Robertson and Dave McKay.

ADAMS, ROBERT.

March 16, 1818. October 30, 1820.
Wife: Mary Adams. Sons: William, Robert, John, Joseph
Adams. Daughters:Ann Brown and Mary Red. Exr: son William.
Wit: Hugh Bennett, Abner Brown and George Whaley.

DICKY, JOHN.

March 13, 1819. March 6, 1820.
Wife: Mary Dicky. Sons: Thomas P., Robert B., John L.
Dicky. Daughters: Agness L., Mary B., Jane, Sarah and
Margaret Dicky. Exrs: son John L. Dicky, Richard Bates
and William Everitt (friend).
Wit: D. Jones, James Hinson and James L. Collins.

MC DONNELL, MARY.

June 28, 1820. March 5, 1821.
Legatees: Samuel B. Simmons (son), Samuel E. Simmons and
Harriet Simmons (a friend). Exr: Samuel B. Simmons (friend).
(Can not explain why Samuel B. Simmons is called son and
is also named as friend). Wit: William Adams, Robert Adams.

MCMANUS, JAMES.

April 20, 1819. December 5, 1820.
Wife: Rebecca McManus. Legatees: wife, Thomas Hugh McManus, Samuel McManus (sons), James McManus (gr.son).

MARTIN, JAMES.

No dates.
Wife: Azilee Martin. Sons: Alexander and William Martin.
Exrs: Jeptha Harrington and Gabril Harrington.
Wit: Alexander Thompson, Harry Thompson, William Thompson.

HANNA, HENRY.

July 26, 1820. March 6, 1821.
Legatees: William Henry Hanna, James Hanna (sons), Eliz-
abeth Hanna, Nancy Elverie Hanna (daughters) and Anna
Hanna (niece). Admrs: Moses Gordon, James Hanna (brother),
John Knox and William H. Hanna (son).
Wit: John Nesmith, Robert Nesmith, Zachariah Nettles.

ANDERSON, JAMES.

November 9, 1822. November 25, 1822.
Wife: Margaret. Son John Anderson. Daughter Mary.
Exr: son John. Wit: Robert H. Gerald, Robert Smith,
John B. Anderson.

DUNN, ROGER.

Probated May 27, 1822.
Wife: Sarah Dunn. Sons: John and Alexander. Daughters:
Mayant Woodward and Fachie. Exr: wife.
Wit: Sutton Capell, James Perkins and W. Roberts.

WALL, HOWELL.

September 21, 1822. October 30, 1822.
All estate to wife Rebra Wall during her life time and
then to legal heirs- not named.
Wit: Drury Wall and Charles Wall.

BROWN, JOHN.

March 17, 1822. April 22, 1822.
Legatees: son Robert Brown, Amelia Hill. Exrs: William
C. McManus and Samuel McManus.
Wit: Gabril Felder, R. Furlow and Benjamin Hill.

LEA, JAMES.

April 6, 1823. April 28, 1823.
Legatees: George, Jesse, David, Alexander, Franklin, Squire
(sons), David Lea (brother), James Lattimore (gr.son),
heirs of daughter Cecelia Lattimore (dec'd.), Sarah
Harper (dau.). Exrs: sons George, Jesse and David.
Wit: W. Boatner, W.R. Naul, Martin Naul.

KEETH, JAMES.

October 25, 1822. April 28, 1823.
Wife: Sarah Keeth. Sons: Lemuel, David and William.
Exr: son Lemuel. Wit: William Gordon, John Campbell
and William Keeth.

TALBERT, JESSE.

August 23, 1822. October 31, 1822.
Sons: Thomas Albert, Silas, Lewis, Abner. Daughter
Mary Montgomery. Exrs: son Abner and Thomas Taylor.
Wit: William Gordon, John Campbell, William Keeth.

DUBOSE, MARY.

September 19, 1821. January 28, 1822.
Daughters: Martha Winans, Mary, Mary Richardson (gr.dau.)
Samuel Dubose (son) and John Dubose (gr.son).
Exrs: William Winans, John G. Richardson, Ira Bowman
(sons-in-law). Wit: Robert Smith and Robert Ne Smith.

GRAY, ROBERT.

May 13, 1822. May 28, 1823.
Legatee: Sarah Penrose (friend and house keeper).
Admr: Daniel Auffman (?), friend.
Wit: Zedekiah Nabor and Rebokaah Nabor.

NEWMAN, JONATHAN.

May 7, 1823. May 26, 1823.
Legatees: son Solomon, Elizabrth Smith, Mary Newman,

heirs of daughter Margarett Armstrong.
Admrs: son Solomon, dau. Mary Newman, William C. Maxwell.
Wit: Benjamin Roberts, Charles W. Knight and David Lea.

EVERITT, JOHN.

October 31, 1821. January 28, 1822.
Wife: Sarah Everitt. Sons: John and Thomas. Daughter:
Martha Wigley. Exrs. sons Thomas and John.
Wit: William Sanders, Nancy Sanders and Thomas Everitt.

JONES, WILLIAM.

February 12, 1821. October 29, 1821.
Wife: Sallie. Sons: Darling, Henry, William, Jonathan,
and Allen. Daughters: Bettie, Emily, Barbara, Aulda
Baker. Exrs: sons, Darling, Henry, William.
Wit: Thomas Lynch, John R. Brown, Steph Strong.

BENNETT, HUGH.

January 20, 1822. January 26, 1824.
Wife: Eliza Bennett. Daughters: Martha, Jean and Julia.
Exrs: wife and Thimas Torrance (friend).

WAGGONER, THOMAS.

May 5, 1824. June 6, 1824.
Wife: Mary Waggoner.Gr.children: Dennis Griffin, Ellis
Griffin, Polly Griffin and Thomas Griffin.
Exrs: wife, David Davis and Sam McManus (friend).
Wit: Archibald Smith, Sarah McManus and Jane Griffin.

CLARK, JOHN M.

January 7, 1824. Jan. 8, 1824.
Legatees: father, mother, brothers and sisters (not
named). Exrs: Darling Jones and John R. Brown.
Wit: I.H. Wright, Eli M. Robinson and John W. Frith.

BRADFORD, SARAH

December 8, 1823. Oct. 24, 1824.
Legatees: neice Rhoda Cates and her children-
Walter Cates, Frances Cates, William Y. Cates (children
of Rhoda Cates), Mary Harrington (dau.of nephew Hezekiah
Harrington). Exrs: Hezekiah Harrington, Gabriel Harrington
(son of Hezekiah). Wit: John Carruth, Sr., Reuben Lee,
John Carruth, Jr.

COLLINS, JAMES L.

December 9, 1823. October 24, 1824.
Legatees:John Collins (brother), Francis Wren (bro.-in-law),
Mehaliea Wren, Althea Spears (sisters)·
Exrs: John Collins and Francis Wren.
Wit: Thomas Torrance, W.C. Maxwell and George Hamlin.

LEA, IVESON G.

September 6, 1824. October 24, 1824.
Wife: Mary Ann Harriett Lea. Exr: Samuel V. Bradley.
Wit: William Lea, Thomas Batghelor (Batchelor),
Steph. H. Strong.

THOMPSON, ALEXANDER.

November 4, 1824. December 27, 1824.
Wife: Une Thompson. Sons: Ephiram, James, Hardy and Will-
iam. Daughter: Mary Watson. Exrs: wife and son William.
Wit: John Carruth,Sr. and Solomon Weathersby.

PITTS, JACOB.

December 13, 1824. March 31, 1825.
Wife: Azilla Pitts. Exr: John Robinson.
Wit: John Robinson and Thomas I. Robinson.

BOWMAN, ELIZABETH.

December 13, 1824. April 26, 1825.
Legatees: son Robert and daughter Eliza.
Wit: Robert Smith and William H. Hanna.

TUCKER, HERBERT.

May 23, 1825. November 16, 1825.
Wife: Lucretia Tucker. Sons: Ivy, Antony and Hillory.
Daughter Kitty. Exrs: wife, Hezekiah Harrington (friend)·
Wit: R.H.C. Pearson and Ezra Cates.

DAVIS, ANN.

July 24, 1825. August 22, 1825.
Legatees: Elijah McKay Davis, Morgan Davis, Stephen R.
Davis (step-sons), Letticea (dau.). Exrs: Elijah M.
Davis, Morgan Davis, Thomas Torrance.
Wit: Solomon Weathersby, John R. Brown, William A. Knox.

LUSK, SAMUEL.

----1815. August 23, 1823.
Wife: Elizabeth Lusk.   Sons: Amos, Joseph, John H.,
Davis. Daughters: Sarah and Lucretia. Executrix: wife.
Wit: Reuben Cassels and Jacob Sojourner.

SHAW, DUNCAN.

March 22, 1822. May 26, 1820.
Legatees: son Jacob and dau. Ann. Wife and other children
mentioned, but not named.
Exr: David Davis. Wit: John Dixon, David Cook, Malcolm
Buie.

BUCKHOLTS, JACOB.

December 27, 1824. August 28, 1826.
Wife: Sarah Buckholts. Sons: William H., Abel H.,
John G. Daughters: Mary, Sarah, Rebecca and Elizabeth.
Exrs: wife, son Abel, John Richards.
Wit: Henry Furlow and James Eversell.

CAMPBELL, JOHN.

August 8, 1826. October 23, 1826.
Sons: William, John, Charles, Lorenzo, Milis, Fletcher.
Exrs: sons William and John.
Wit: James Denman, William Gardner, Elizabeth Kennon.

KNOX, SAM M.

June 11, 1826. October 22, 1826.
Wife: Ann Knox. Son Samuel Knox. Exrs: wife, Richard
Hunt. Wit: Charles McKnight, Leonora Wetherspoon.

MILLER, JAMES.

July 4, 1826. December 29, 1827.
Wife Lydia and children. Exrs: sons Moses and Aaron.
Wit: Obed Mixon and J. Holden.

EVERETT, ALEXANDER B.

February 11, 1828. April 30, 1828.
Wife: Elizabeth Everett. Daughters: Julia Ann, Mary,
Eliza and Nancy. Son Henry. Executrix: wife.
Wit: William Everett, Thomas Everett, John Everett.

GAYLE, JOSIAH.

---------July 13, 1828.
Legatees: wife and children- not named.
Exrs: wife, son Joseph and Isaac Caulifield.
Wit: Benjamin M. Graves and David Pemble.

ARNOLD, ISOM.

November, 1827. January 16, 1828.
Executrix and legatee : wife Mary.
Wit: James Parson, James Adams, Jesse Graves.

CAUSEY, WILLIAM.

July 3, 1828. July 21, 1828.
Wife: Susan. Sons: Alexander, Seaborn, Truant, Zachariah, Solomon, Jonas, Thomas, John, and gr.son John M. Daniel.
Daughters: Anna, Cynthia, Betty.
Wit: Thomas Toler, Philip Huff, David Cox.

ANDERSON, JOHN.

Sept. 1, 1828.
Legatees: Margaret Anderson (mother), Mary McRae (sister).
Executrix: mother. Wit: John Smylie, Thomas Lyne.

FRITH, JOHN E.

Jan. 20, 1829. May 19, 1829.
Wife: Mary Frith. Sons: John and William. Daughter: Rebecca. Exrs: wife and son Herbert.
Wit: Morgan Davis, Ed Carroll, V.T. Crawford.

CROPPER, JAMES M.

February 8, 1829. May 5, 1829.
Legatee: William Cropper (brother).
Exr: Ira Bowman (friend). Wit: A.M. Dunn, A.C.Dunn.

WAIT, JOHN.

March 8, 1829. May 18, 1829.
Legatees: wife Elizabeth and children.
Exrs: Robert Longmire, Thomas Goode.
Wit: Stephen Wilkinson and William Goode.

BROWNE JOHN RAY.

March 19, 1829. September 16, 1829.
Legatees: Arminda and Chlorenda (daughters), Solomon Weathersby (friend). Exrs: Solomon Weathersby, Gabriel Fol-
der and William Stewart (true friends).
Wit: William Lea, Minor M. Whitney and John Hale.

SWEARINGEN, HENRY.

June 20, 1829. September 21, 1829.
Sons: Thomas, John, Henry. Daughter Elizabeth.
Exrs: Thomas Swearingen (father) and John Swearingen.
Wit: Solomon Weathersby and David McGeehee.

MORGAN WILLIAM.

May 28, 1830. June 21, 1830.
Wife: Elizabeth. Sons: Willie, Hiram, James, Fielden,
Benjamin and John. Daughter: Elizabeth. Delana (a child).
Exrs: wife and son Willie.
Wit: Thomas Batchelor, Griffen Gayden and William Spinks.

BUCKHOLTS, JOHN G.

Sept. 4, 1830. September 20, 1830.
Wife: Adaline. Sons: Charles B. and John A. Daughters:
Elizabeth and Martha A.
Exrs: wife, Charles Davis.
Wit: Gab Felder, S. Botters and S.H. Strong.

JENKINS, WILLIE.

April 19, 1828. September 20, 1830.
Legatees: wife (not named), Elizabeth Whittington (sister), James and William Jenkins (sons).
Exr: son James. Wit: John Hutchins, Edmond Hutchins
and Daniel Rainer.

RAIFORD, THOMAS.

September 28, 1830. October 18, 1830.
Sons: William F. and Thomas W. Raiford. Dau: Sarah Ann.
Exrs: James G. Garner and Wilfor Garner (friends).
Wit: Sol Weathersby, Elijah Martin and Philip R. Jones.

ROBINSON, MOSES.

October 7, 1830. December 20, 1830.
Wife: Temperance . Sons: John and Andrew. Gr.daus: Eliza-
beth and Matilda Jones. Exrs. James and Wilfor Garner.
Wit: Sol Weathersby, Elijah Martin, Philip R. Jones.

CHANDLER, JAMES.

March 24, 1830. Jan. 31, 1831.
Children: James, Catherine and children of dau. Martha
Burris (dec'd). Exrs: Elias Norwood (son-in-law) and
Samuel B. Simmons (stepson).
Wit: John C. Wilson, Enos Burris, Stephen H. Strong.

LOWRY, WILLIAM.

Probated April 6, 1831.
Sons: John and William. Daughters: Elizabeth, Martha
and Emiline. Exrs: sons John and William, Thomas Torrance
(brother-in-law). Wit: Thomas Torrance, Margaret Bennett
and Minerva Torrance.

TERRELL, MOSES.

January 4, 1828. February 21, 1831.
Wife: Nancy. Sons: John and Hiram Terrell. Daughter
Rebecca. Exrs: sons Hiram and Elijah.
Wit: W.T. Crawford, Gab Felder and Benjamin Wall.

CAPELL, LITTLETON.

May 7, 1830. June 20, 1831.
Wife: Catherine. Son: Eli, gr.son John Caldwell.
Daughters: Julia, Nancy, Elizabeth, Eze.
Exrs: F.Reuben Smith, Jesse Knighten, Eli Capell.
Wit: A.M. Dunn, L.S. Wilkinson, David Kinebrew.

BURRIS, ENOS.

September 13, 1831. October 17, 1831.
(Of Louisana). Legatees: Addison, Hampton, George and
James Burris (brothers), Harriet Simmons (sister).
Wit: Edwin Collins, John Whitaker, Thomas Hamilton and
John A. Hamilton.

HUFF, BENJAMIN.

October 1, 1831. November 4, 1831.
Wife: Sarah Huff. Sons: Newton, Robert and Howell.
Daughters: Elizabeth and Letitia. Exr: Thomas Talbert
(brother-in-law). Wit: Aaron Butler, Garnet Briant and
Angus Wilkinson.

LARD, THOMAS.

Sept. 3, 1831. Oct.17, 1831.
Sons: Ephiram, Henry and Gideon.
Exrs: Samuel B. Simmons. Wit: John Crossley, John Cockerham.

MOREHOUSE, JACOB.

Oct. 18, 1831. January 31, 1832.
Legatees: Children of a friend, John Rollins of Louisana,
- Fletcher, May Ann, William and David Rollins.
Exrs: William Lattimore, Barnabas Pipkin (of La.)
Wit: James Williams, James Lattimore, William Lattimore.

SWEARINGEN, JOEL.

January 1, 1832. June 19, 1832.
Wife: Susan. Sons: Samuel, Abel C., William and George W.
Exrs: son Abel C. and Richard Bates ("trusty friend").

RICE, JESSE.

May 20, 1831. January 9, 1832.
Wife: Frances. Sons: John, Robert and James Rice.
Exr: wife. Wit: Thomas Loudner, Francis Wren, Robert Cox.

EVERETT, WILLIAM.

May 221 1832. August 20, 1832.
Legatees: Henry Richard Everett and heirs, James Everett
(brother), John Everett (nephew) and Elizabeth Gibson
and heirs. Exrs: Henry Richard Everett (nephew) and John
Everett. Wit: John W. Page, Thomas Cockram, Benjamin
Tarver.

RABORN, ANTHONY.

Sept. 14, 1832. October 15, 1832.
Legatees: wife Nancy and son Willie, other minor children mentioned, but not named.
Exrs: wife, Lewis Raborn. Wit: Jehu Wall, Howell Wall
and James Strickland.

TOLER, THOMAS.

Probated September 22, 1833.
Wife: Margaret. Sons: Joel, Thomas, Tillman. Daughters:
Milly, Magdalena, Sarah, Elizabeth and Susanna.
Exrs: to be appointed by the Probate Judge.
Wit: W. Jackson, Lewis Jackson, Joel Toler.

RABORN, GEORGE.

August 15, 1827.   November 18, 1833.
Legatees: wife Rachel and several children, not named.
Exrs: wife and Joseph Raborn,Sr.
Wit: Obed Mixon, Benhadade Mixon and Michael Mixon.

DAVIS, CHARLES.

December 25, 1833. January 21, 1834.
Legatees: Victoria (dau.), Elizabeth Brown (sister).
Exrs: Thomas Batchelor, Agrippa Gayden.
Wit: William Stewart, John Wall, W.H. Dillenham.

WILKINSON, MICAYAH.

May 7, 1806. September 7, 1826.
Of Adams County, Miss. Legatees: wife and children (not
named). Exrs: none named. Wit: Joseph Erwin, James Erwin
and Zadock Boman.

ROBINSON, JAMES.

May 6, 1834.   July 21, 1834.
Wife: Catherine. Sons: Allen, Reason and Moses.
Daughters: Emily and Catherine. Exrs: wife, son Allen
and William Baker (friend). Wit: Robert Stewart, Robert
Wilson and Charles McClain.

GARNER, JAMES.

February 19, 1832.   August 20, 1834.
Wife: Sarah.   Sons: Thomas, Oliver, James, Sedford
and Wilford. Exrs: wife and son Wilford.
Daughters: Maryanna, Elizabeth and Sarah.
Wit: James Denman, Allen Spurlock, Elizabeth Denman.

CRUSE, ELIZABETH.

November 27, 1833.   August 17, 1833.
Legatees: Frances Marsh, Frances Mely Marsh (nieces)
and Robert Marsh (brother). Exr: John B. Swearingen.
Wit: Thomas Swearingen, V.F. Swearingen.

LARD, JOHN.

March 30, 1835. August 17, 1835.
Brother Gideon Lard and cousin Joseph Lard named as
legatees and Exrs.
Wit: John Crossley, James R. Robinson and John Cockerham.

FAUST, M.S.

March 2, 1835. September, 1835
Wife: Margarett. Sons: James, David, J.P. Daughters:
Loretta, Sarah, Nancy, Rachel, Octavo and Margarett.
Exrs: wife and David Cox.
Wit: Philip R. James, Nicy James, James McDowell.

ANDERSON, MARGARETT.

August 23, 1835. September 23, 1835.
Legatees: Mary McRae (dau.), David Anderson, James Frier-
son, Margarett Flemon, Charles Way, William Way, Harry
Cage, Griffin P. Clanghton and Elsa, Josiah and Lenah
(3 slaves to be free).
Exrs: Harry Cage and Griffin P. Clanghton.
Wit: John B. Anderson, Lawerence Anderson, Jeremiah Brewer.

PADELFORD, WILLIAM T.

November 15, 1835. December 2, 1835.
Children: Mary Adaline, Theodore and Hariett.
Exrs: Robert B. Dickey.
Wit: H.R. Everett, Robert B. Dickey, Zachens Lard.

BOATNER, ELIAS.

September 2, 1833. December 22, 1835.
Wife: Jane. Sons: Ezekiel, Daniel, Mark and gr.son Elias
Boatner. Exrs: none named. Wit: David Pemble, Jacob Boat-
ner and Thomas C. Black.

KINNEBREW, DAVID.

Probated May 19, 1835.
Wife: Sarah. Sons: John, Marshall, Orlander, James, Will-
iam, Leonard and Lattimore.
Exrs: David Davis, John Gunby Reese.
Wit: C.Sam Houston, Nathaniel Smiley, Robert P. Smiley.

MOORE, SAMUEL.

September 2, 1835. Jan. 18, 1836.
Wife: mentioned, but not named. Children: John, William,
Allen, Thomas, Martha and unborn child.
Exrs: John Moore, Thomas S. Moore.
Wit: Ludwick Weathersby, Solomon Weathersby, William Adams.

STRONG, STEPHEN.

March 26, 1836. April 11, 1836.
Legatees: Susannah Strong (mother), sisters Jane, Eliza,
Margarett, Sarah, Susan. Exrs: Thos. Cheatham, Fr. Wren.

MCRAE, WILLIAM.

April 4, 1836. June 6, 1836.
Wife· Mary McRae. John McRae, William Archard and Robert
Archard (nephews). Exrs: Jones Stewart and David Pemble.
Wit: John B. Anderson and Abner J. Gunter.

HALFORD, JACOB.

September 16, 1834. August 22, 1836.
Legatees: wife Susannah and children of John Terrell.
Wit: T.J. Spurlock, E.M. Davis and V.T. Crawford.

RHODES, CHARLES.

January 16, 1837. January, 1837.
Wife: Olivia Rhodes. Rebecca Webb and Elizabeth Smith
(daughters). Exr: Charles Rhodes Webb (gr.son).
Wit: John H. Nunnery and George W. Griffin.

BROKUS, WILLIAM, SR.

Oct. 5, 1805. Dec. 30, 1805
To only daughter, Annie, plantation where I now live,
7 slaves, horses, cows, colts etc.
Grandsons: Stephen and William Minor, to have property
after decease of daughter Annie.
John Brokus (son of nephew William Brokus), to have $500.
Exrs: Benjamin Beek, Thomas Calvit, William Brokus,Jr.,
Stephen Minor. Wit: Daniel Burnet, Thomas White, Samuel
Bridgers, John Booth, J. Eldergill.

ROSS, SARAH.

---1806. Feb. Court, 1806.
Daughters: Elizabeth Rapalje and Rebecca Marshall.
Exr: Elizabeth Rapalje. Wit: James Sampson, Kak Moor.

QUILLING, MOSES.

Nov. 17, 1805. July 30, 1806.
Exr. and Legatee: Hezekiah Harmon.
Wit: Elisha Flower, Benjamin Ketching, William Lincoln.

MCELWEE, JAMES.

March 12, 1806. August Court, 1806.
Wife: Mary Mc Elwee. Sons: James, David and Stephen.
Daughters: Elizabeth, Margaret, Fanny and Mary.
Exrs: wife, William Tabor, Samson Corbin.
Wit: Josiah Arundell, Isaac Clark.

MILLER, WILLIAM.

May 28, 1806.   August Court, 1806.
Estate bequeathed to wife and youngest children (not
named). Mentions oldest married children, but does
not name. Exr: James Booth.
Wit: Matt Turney, James S. Dearmond, John Cross, Joseph
Bates.

CHAMBLIS, WILLIAM.

Wife: Rebecca Chamblis. Daughter: Ann Chamblis.
Wit: J.A. Maxwell, P.A.Vandone, John B. Cobun.

BLAND, ISAAC.

March 8, 1820-   ----------
Wife: Jane Bland. Son: Maxwell Washington Bland.
Exrs: wife, Benjamin Smith.
Wit: Lack P. Gee, Joseph Bullard, Philip Alston.

MCALLISTER, HECTOR.

May 27, 1820. --------
Wife: Mary McAllister. Sons: Duncan and John McAllister.
Daughters: 5 --but not named.
Exrs: wife, John McAllister, Daniel McAllister.
Wit: William Harvey, John Hays, Daniel Lamont, Daniel
McAllister.

------JOSEPH.

Probated Nov. 12, 1803.
Wife: Molly, to have 1/3 of estate and 2 slaves.
Children: mentioned, but not named.
Wit: Duncan Cameron, Joseph Ballard, George Eslinger.

ROSS, JOHN.

August 18, 1803. Feb. 4, 1804.
Estate to mother, after her decease to sister, Eliza-
beth Rapalje. Exrs: Isaac Rapalje, Sarah Stowers.
Wit: Vincent Fortner, Thomas Fortner, William Mathews.

EVANS, GEORGE.

March 18, 1802. November Court, 1804. Of Southwest Ter.
Wife: Martha, to have slaves, furniture and money.
Sons: Thomas and Ezekiel, to have money and slaves.
Daughters: Jemima, Rebekah and Ann Jean.
Wit: Jesse Griffin, Robert Moor, Gideon James.

WHITE, THOMAS, SR.

Feb. 21, 1803. Oct. 6, 1804.
Son Thomas White and his wife, Sarah, to have slaves.
Estate to be divided between : Lucy Angle, Joseph White,
Rachel Parks, Mildred Hightower, Thomas White, Susanna
Henson, Hirtley Baker, Agnes Simpson, save ten shillings

to sons Benjamin and Reuben White.
Exrs: son Thomas White and Samuel Gibson.
Wit: Gideon James, Julius Smith, Jesse Griffin.
Probated before Samuel Bridgers, Chief Justice for
County of Claiborne.

GIBSON, TOBIAS.

August 2, 1803. August Court, 1804.
Legatees: Rhody Gibson, to have a saddle horse;
nephews- Nathaniel (son of Nath'l. Gibson, dec'd.),
Tobias (son of Mallicq(?), dec'd.), Jordan (son of Stephen Gibson), all stock and horses.Slaves, Joe and Doll,
to have their freedom. Exr: Stephen Gibson.
Wit: Shelly Booth, Joseph Ferguson, Seth Caston.

LIVINGSTON, PETER VAN BURGH.

Sept. 10, 1792. --------(Late of New York, now of Eliz-
abethtown, New Jersey)· Wife: Elizabeth. Son: Philip.
Daughters: Catherine Bayard and Sarah Ricketts.
Legatees: George Van Burgh Brown (son of dau. Mary);
Mary (dau. of son Peter, dec'd.); Susan Livingston (wid-
ow of son Peter); Elizabeth Otto.
Exrs: Gerard Bancher (Treasurer of State of New York)
and son Philip Livingston. (A long codicil to this will).

MONTGOMERY, JOSEPH.

Probated Nov. 1825.
Wife: Mary. Children mentioned, but not named.
Exrs: wife, Parmenias Briscoe.
Wit: William Walker, William Cook, John Rundell.

KING, WILLIAM.

At a court held in Washington County (Virginia ?), Dec.
20, 1808, the will of William King was probated. Proved
by the oaths of James King, William Trigg and William
D. Nelson, Executors. Will was made March 3, 1806.
Col. James King, Samuel King, Jacob Baker said the will
and codicil, of date of 3 March, 1806, are in the hand
writing of said William King. William Trigg and James
Trigg took oaths as Executors, as prescribed by law,
and entered into and acknowledged their bond in the sum
of $1,500,000, with Robert Craig, Jr., Thomas Tate, Rob-
ert D. Delays, John Aperson, Joseph Cole, Robert White
Bascolm Talbott, John Cole, Thomas Moffett, Joshua Banks,
William Duff, William Jones, Benjamin Estill, Samuel Vance,
James Bryant, Michael Shaves, Gerard T. Come, James Thomp-

son, Enoch Schoolfield, GeorgeSpangler, James Keys, John
McCullock,,John Willis, William Gray, James Lyon, Alex-
ander Hamilton, Benjamin Longley, Jacob Munglly, Robert
Huston, Reuben Bradley, Val. Baugh, John Mitchell, Jacob
Baker, John McCormack, Robert Craig, John Athey, John
Goodson, Peter Clark, John Buchanan, James King, Sr.,
Samuel Meek, Samuel Glenn, Rufus Morgan, James Angley,
William McHenry, Michael Deschert, Lilburn Henderson,
John J.Trigg, David Smith, Robert Duke, William Nelson,
Jacob Long, Welcome Martin, Robert McCullock, Thomas
Thornburg, Benjamin Clark, Michael Willoughby, Conley
Findley, William King, Jacob Miller, Charles Tate,
William Poston, Peter Scott.
A certificate is granted them for probate of said will,
December 29, 1808.

BARNES, JOSIAH.

September 7, 1810. Feb. 13, 1811.
Wife: Esther Barnes, to have slaves, plantation,
and personal estate. Legatees: Martha Willis (dau.),
to have $1., having received her share; son William,
to have $1.; Nancy Flowers (dau.) to have personal
estate; Benjamin Bryan Barnes (gr.son); Polly Barnes.
Rest of estate to be divided between sons Joseph, Lewis
and Elias and daughters Helen, Susan, Sally, Harriett,
Asenath Barnes. Exrs: Ignatius Flowers (son-in-law)
and Thomas Barnes.
Wit: Samuel Cobun, Everitt Lee, Ansell Towell.

THOMAS, WILLIAM.

October 5, 1810. Feb. 14, 1812.
Wife: Elizabeth, to have slaves.
Daughters: Louisana Burch, to have slaves; Jane Kit-
crease, slaves ; Patsy Thomas, slaves ; Eleanor Thomas,
slaves: Sons: Thomas C.L. (youngest son), to have
slaves; Knowland, William, Frances Spann Thomas to have
real estate. Exrs: sons Knowland and William.
Wit: James Triaro (?) and Henry Milburne.

RITCHEY, DANIEL.

April 14, 1813. August, 1813.
Wife: to have furniture and household goods.
Son: Leonard.   Exrs: Walter Leake, Henry Johnston.
Wit: Davenport Wisemaud, Joel White, John Deanis.

McCALEB, WILLIAM.

March 5, 1813. August 9, 1813.

Wife: to have slaves.
Youngest daughter, Jane McCalob, to have furniture and
slaves. Sons: James, David, John, Jonathan.

BRASHEARS, MARTHA.

Nov. 15, 1813. Nov. 15, 1814.
Sons: Turner Bolt, Tobias Eden, Mershane Franklin, all
to have slaves. Daughters: Priscilla Brashears and Lucy
Lee, to have slaves. Faithful old servant Peter, to have
his freedom. Exrs: David Lee, Isaac Repalje, Teisilla
Brashear. Wit: Thomas Fortner, William E. Campbell,
Lain Cloyd.

WOOLDRIDGE, WILLIAM H.

April 18, 1810. May 1814.
Wife: Nancy, to have all land and real estate in Territory.
Son: Elam Sparks Wooldridge, to have land and slaves.
Exr: Richard Sparks. Wit: Samuel Frye, Ruth Sparks and
Mary Milliken.

ROBINSON, SETH.

Probated June 5, 1814.
Legatees: Mary Robinson (mother), of Chester County, Penn.
to have $1,000 ; sister Hannah Cox (wife of John Cox);
Amey Roberts; Polly Way (wife of John Way); Elizabeth
Robinson, Ann Robinson and Lydia Robinson- sisters to have
$150. each, residue to be divided between brothers Jo-
seph and William Robinson, brothers also to have $300. each.
Wit: Samuel Gibson, Robert Steele, Jeff H. Moore.

MOORE, JEFF F.

25 October, 1813. Formerly of Chester County, Penn.
Estate bequeathed to brothers: Joseph, Ermer, James and
sister Eliza Taylor Moore. Sister Eliza to have paint
box. Nephews: Robert Feager Moore and Joseph Moore.
Exrs: Joseph Moore and Ermer Moore.
Wit: Joseph Briggs, Ralph Rogan, Thomas T. Swann.

EVANS, THOMAS.

June 12, 1813. August, 1813.
Wife: Catherine, to have land and care of children.
Children: Harriett, John, Jarett, Jane and Addie Evans.
Exrs: James Archer, Col. David Burnet, William Neeley.
Wit: John Robertson, W. B. Minor, James Archer.

WHITE, THOMAS.

July 30 ,1812. Jan. 16, 1813.
Wife: Sarah White, to have 1/3 of estate.
Sons: Nelson and Thompson, to have land.
The following children are to have share and share alike:
Larkin, Nelson, Sophia Sims, Thompson , Sarah White, Jo-
seph and Benjamin. Exrs: son Nelson and Ralph Rejan.

COBUN, SAMUEL.

Jan. 28, 1813. Feb. 9, 1813.
Sisters: Elizabeth and Nancy Cobun.
Daughters: Kitty and Mary Cobun, to have personal prop-
erty. Sons: Samuel and John Cobun.
Exrs: Daniel Burnet, Samuel Gibson.

MANNING, SILAS.

April 25, 1813. May 10, 1813.
Estate to be divided between the children of H. Harmon-
Polly, Rebecca, Elizabeth, James and Joseph Harmon.
Exr: Hezekiah Harmon. Wit: Catherine Harmon, Clemore Bogs.

FOSTER, WILLIAM.

Dec.3, 1808. Feb. 10, 1810.
Daughters: Sally Smith, Eliza Heath, Polly Smith,
Phebe Catuchead (?), Rutha Foster, Patsy Foster, Rebecca
Foster, all to have slaves.   Sons: Truett, to have slaves;
James, land; Spencer, land; Shadrack Foster.
Exrs: William Johnson, John Slaughter.
Wit: John Slaughter.

BULLOCK, STEPHEN.

Jan. 3, 1812. March 4, 1812.
"I request that my Executors have the best education given
my children, that the most enlightened seminaries of the
United States can afford, and circumstances of my estate
warrant." Exrs: Thomas Mar and Abraham Barnes.
Wit: J. Buchan, Peter Lamm, Thomas Barnes.

VANCE, THOMAS.

September 7, 1804. Nov. 11, 1805.
Wife: Elizabeth, to have use of plantation until youngest daughter, Bridget, arrives at the age of fifteen years,
then 1/2 of plantation during widowhood; at the death or
marriage of my widow, her share to go to Ephiram Vance.

Children: Ephiram, William, Mary, other children mentioned
but not named. Exrs: wife, Jesse Griffin.
Wit: Isaac and Nancy Fife.

MANDELL, ANDREW.

Jan. 23, 1817.
Wife: Polly Mandell. Children: Abijah Hunt, Joseph,
Frances· Younger children (not named) have gift of prop-
erty from their uncle, Stephen Minor. Exr: wife.
Wit: G.W.Humphrey, James Crane, D.G.Humphrey.

BARNES, THOMAS.

March 17, 1817.
Wife: Mary· Children: Martha White, John Alexander, Susan,
Alfred, Nancy and Elizabeth. Exrs: wife, John A. Barnes,
Nelson White. Wit: Abraham Barnes, Merrell Rowland, Thom-
as Bridger.

WALLACE, DANIEL.

Oct. 9, 1818.   ------
Legatees: Elizabeth Mealey and her children.
Wit: A.D. Dillingham, Elliott Nigles.
Exr: Stephen D. Carson.

SMITH, JOSHUA.

Nov. 30, 1817.
Wife: Jane and youngest daughter to have estate- other
children mentioned, but not named. Exr: wife.
Wit: Ezra Marble, R.A.Ree (?).

MOOR, ROBERT.

Nov. 24, 1817. -----
Wife: Samoine (?)·
Daughters: Sally, Elizabeth, Nancy, Polly, Alicy (step-
dau.). Sons: Calvin, Allen, James, William.
Wit: W.C.Buchan, J. Buchan.

GIBSON, SAMUEL.

--------   ------
Daughter: Rebecca Gibson, to have one lot of ground in
the suburbs of Gibson Fort. Sons: John G. Gibson, Robert Frazer Moor Gibson· Daus: Nancy Minor and Rebecca.
Exrs: son John, Dr. Joseph Moor, William King.

FREELAND, FRISBY.

August 24, 1815. -------
Legatees: Thomas Freeland (son); Augustus Freeland (son);
children of daughter Rebecca Chew; Elizabeth C.G.Williamson
(gr.dau); Sarah Frisby Freeland (gr.dau.); Edward R.I.
Allnict (nephew); mentions money to be paid estate, in
Maryland. Exrs: Waterman Crane, Robert Crane, James
Crane.

HARMON, JAMES.

Sept. 16, 1817. ---------
Legatees: Silence (dau.), wife of Elisha Flowers; Lavina
(dau.-dec'd.), who was wife of William Tabor; dau. Lydia,
wife of Joshua Aaron, dec'd.; dau. Abial (dec'd), wife
of Josiah Flowers; James and Joseph Harmon (gr.sons).
Exr: son Hezikiah.
Wit: John Goodhorne, Nancy Hamilton, Philenia Brooks.

JONES, SUSANNAH.

October 1, 1819.--------
Legatees: Nelson Thomas, Rachel Parks, Elizabeth Parks,
Susan Clark. Exr: William Dunn.
Wit: James Wadlington, D.S.Jones, Mary Allen, S.Allen.

WHITE, LARKINS.

Feb. 10, 1820. -------
Children: Louisa and William White.
Exrs: Jeremiah McCaleb, Ralph Ragan.
Wit: William McGreon, J.A.Denny, Joe Bell.

WELLS, WILLIAM.

October 23, 1819.
Son: James Well.   Wife: Mildred Wells.
Exrs: wife, Henry Johnson, Alsalom Bobo.
Wit: Philip Alorton, William Bassett, Elijah Ragsdale.

WISEMAN, D.

February 2, 1820.
Wife: Sophia Wiseman. Exrs: Larkin White, Ralph Regan.
Wit: Phil Alston, Ralph Regan, Larkin White, Phebe Regan.

MINOR, STEPHEN.

Legatees : **wife, Ann, and her heirs.**
Exrs: Joseph Moore and John Gibson.
Wit: Elias Ogden, A.G. Gage, Orran Faulk.
July 7, 1821.

WILLIS, WILLIAM.

No date prob. 1821.
Legatees: Martha (wife); John (son); Nancy and Harriett
(sisters; Thomas and Daniel Willis (brothers); Sarah
Voss (niece); Eliza Loybourne (niece).

DAVIS, REUBEN.

March 8, 1821.
Children: John I., Betsy Fisher, William, James, Joseph,
Septha, Adin, Ator. Exrs: Sarah Davis (wife), son Will-
iam. Wit: Phil Alston.

FLOWERS, ELISHA.

August 2, 1816.
Wife: Silence Flowers. Legatees: Elisha and Samuel
Flowers (nephews); Sally Kitchens, Lucy Sturdivant,
Elizabeth Walker, Nancy Flowers, Samuel Flowers.
Exrs: Elisha and Josiah Flowers.
Wit: Tobias Cummings and John Garvek (?)

LANE, WILLIAM.

No dates. of Charlestown, S.C.
Wife: Elizabeth
Children: James, Abraham, Betsy, Hannah, Mary and Will-
iam. Exr: brother-in-law Eskrolls, of S.C.
Wit: William Tuttle, Thomas Morris.

COUREY, WILLIAM.

July 9, 1808.
Children: William (oldest), Elizabeth Courey, Thomas
Jefferson, Stephen and Jackson.
Exrs: Lewis Courey, John Turnbull, Ezekiel Young.
Wit: William Davis, William Robinson, Ezekiel Young.

EVANS, W.O.

June 3, 1822.
Children: Arthur Evans, Balsore Evans (dau.).
Wit: Charlotte Evans, William Low, Martha Cooper.

CAFFERY, MARY.

June 20, 1820. -------
Sons: John and Jefferson Caffery. Granddau: Rachel Wal-
ker.   Exr: Peter Vandown.
Wit: A. Green, David Walker, Thomas Green, Elizabeth
Green.

PRINCE, BAYLISS E.

1825-----
Wife: Catherine Shelby Prince. Son: William.
Land to children of deceased brother and sister.
Exrs: wife and bro. William.
Wit: William Terry, Andrew Ellis, N. Jefferson.

CRANE, WATERMAN.

Feb. 5, 1826.
Wife: Catherine. Legatees: William Crane and Robert Mitchell (gr.sons); James Crane (son); Lucy McNeil and Clarissa Young (daus.); Caroline Christian and Catherine Quinn
(gr.daus.). Exrs: wife, James Crane, William Young.

HOBERT, ZEBULON.

Nov. 1819.
Daughters: Susannah and Hester.
Wit: William Dunn, Jackson Dunn.

KNOWLTON, JOHN.

Sept. 12, 1819.
Estate to "my little friends, Esther Ann King and William
Armstrong King". (Children of William King)
Exrs: William King and Eli Montgomery.
Wit: T.B.Minor, John B. Cobun.

CLARK, GIBSON.

Feb. 23, 1823. ----
Legatees: Piety and Rosannah Gibson Clark (daus. of son
Gibson Clark); Elijah Clark and Gibson Clark Heddrick(gr·
sons); Elizabeth Susan Piety and Sarah Stellar, daus.
of Mary Stellar (dau.); Nancy Heddrick (dau.); Elijah
and William (sons); Elizabeth Minor (gr.dau.).
Exrs: sons Gibson and Elijah P. , John Heddrick.
Wit: Julius Bettiz, Reuben Spear, James Perry and Dan
Burnet.

FRAZER, ELIPHAET.

March 26, 1816.
"To embark soon for the eastern states of America."
Legatees: Betsy Frazer (wife); Eliza Frazer (dau.);
Roe (nephew), to have $1000 : daughter to have 1/2 of
estate. Should a son be born I want him named for bro.
James· Should wife and daughter not survive, then sister,
Eliza Lord, to have 1/10 of estate, and father, James
Frazer, to have balance for use during his life, then it
is to go to sister, Phebe Rea.
Exrs: wife, Daniel Virtner.
Wit: William R. McAlpine, John B. Cobun.

SAXON, JOSHUA.

January 31, 1817.
Wife: Medas (or Medar)· Sons: Orville, Millbourne (young-
est), Joshua, Jr.
Daughters: Charlotte Ingram, Lucinda Miller, Clarinda
Anderson, Nancy Anderson and Malinda Terry.
Exrs: Joshua Saxon, Jr., Robert Caldwell, Medar Saxon.
Wit: P. Griffin, Moses Sheay, John F. McCae.

SPARKS, RICHARD.

March 6, 1814. October 9, 1815.
Wife: Ruth, to have land and a large number of slaves·
Legatees: dau. Polly Hall, land in Tenn.; dau. Catherine
McClure, land on the east fork of Miaume, in State of Ohio;
dau. Charity Cooper, to have land in Pennsylvania; daus.
Elizabeth Besagrade (?) and Eleanor Sparks, to have 600
acres in Tenn.; Capt. George W. Seveir (friend), to have
my gold headed cane; Thomas D. and Stephen Carson, to
have all my military apparel; Stephen Carson, "my rifle
gun, it being my support in youth and can --(?) in old
age; Edward Sparks Wooldridge, son of late Col. William
Wooldridge, a lot.
Exrs: wife, Daniel Vertner, Stephen Carson.
Wit: James Lee, Stephen Carson, George K. Cook.

KENDALL, JOSHUA.

May 3, 1816. May Court, 1816.
Wife: Rachel, and children mentioned, but not named.

ARCHER, JAMES.

May 14, 1815.-------
Wife: mentioned, but not named. Legatees: Capt. Isaac
Ross (father-in-law); Martha Ross (sister-in-law);

John Evatt (friend), watch; brother John Archer, $500.;
mentions 3 other brothers- Thomas, Robert, Stevenson.
Exrs: Capt. Isaac Ross, John Evatt.
Wit: J. Moore, D. Downing, Frances Griffin.

PATTERSON, JOHN.

Wife: Jane Patterson. Exrs: wife, Daniel Burnet, Sam -
uel Cobun. Wit: Orran Faulk, Alfred Faulk, Josiah Newman.

HARRIS, CLAIBORNE.

August 24, 1821.
Daughter: Melbina· Son: Henderson Harris.
Exr: Dr. David Downey. Wit: Jesse Mabry, James Watson.

GRONINGER, GEORGE.

July 25, 1821.
Legatee: Fred Strauss· Wit: William Walker.

COOPER, WILLIAM.

December 14, 1822.
Exrs: Mabon Cooper, Claiborne Cooper (son).
Children: mentioned, but not named.
Wit: R.S.Caldwell, Solomon Cooper.

BASSETT, WILLIAM.

May 24, 1823.----
Legatees: Huston Bassett (half brother); Penelope Jones
(half sister); other brothers mentioned, but not named;
Sarah Davis, Jeremiah and Alfred Robinson, cousins.
Wit: Sulton Byrd, Benjamin Mitchell, Daniel Burnett.

FLOWERS, NACY.

April 8, 1823.
Exr. and Wife: Huldy, and children (not named).
Wit: P. Briscoe, Polly Harris, Amanda Liggett.

MCALPEN, ALEXANDER.

May 26, 1823.
Daniel and Duncan McAlpen, only children mentioned.
Exrs: Duncan McAlpen and John McAlpen.

RAGSDALE, SAMUEL.

No dates.
Wife: Anna. Legatees: Edward Ragsdale, Nancy B. Truly,
Patsy Crane, John M. Ragsdale, Francis Ragsdale (prob.
children of Samuel Ragsdale); William Ragsdale (son).
Exr: son John Ragsdale.
Wit: G. Keirn, William Daniel, Elijah Ragsdale.

CLARKE, ELIJAH.

September 8, 1823. ------
Children: Piety, John, Lawerence, Lucinda, Elijah Raymond
Clarke. John Robinson, to have charge of the children.
Brother: Lewis Clarke.   Exr: David McCaleb.
Wit: Raymond Robinson, John Robinson, Henry Johnston.

ROUSH, JOHN.

March 25, 1826.
Legatee and Exr: John D. Zeizer.
Wit: Evan Griffith, John H. Estey.

BARNES, JOSEPH.

March 8, 1824. ---
Legatees: sisters- Susan and Harriett and brother Elias
Barnes. Wit: J. Moore, Samuel Cobun, James Moore.

GIBSON, JAMES.

October 3, 1822.
Wife: Elizabeth Gibson. Children: Levi, Clarke, Nancy.
Tersea Caroline McGinty (niece of my wife and dau. of
Reuben McGinty). Exrs: Joseph Pumly, John A. Gibson,
Levi Gibson. Wit: Samuel Gibson, Randol Gibson and
John A. Gibson.

SCOTT, WILLIAM.

October 25, 1825.
Wife: Margaret, to be guardian of children(not named).
Exrs: wife, Isarel Loring, Daniel Vertner, A.W.Putnam,
Pete Vandone, Abraham Barnes.
Wit: Thomas Cotton, James Sharo, James Cotton.

BOOTH, JOHN,SR.

January 14, 1824.

Wife: Hester Booth. Daughters: Charlotte Clark, Lydia
Truly, Elizabeth Wright, Hester Deen. Son: John Booth,Jr.
Gr.children: John Barcus (or Brocus), William Barcus,
Hester Barcus, and my great-grandchildren (not named).
Exrs: son John, Daniel Burnett.
Wit: Cornelius Haring and Eleazer Haring.

BRIMSON, GAUSE.

May 25, 1825.
Wife: Jane Brimson· Children: men'tioned, but not named.
Exrs: wife, Ambrose Barnes, Adam Gordon.

SMITH, CELIAB.

June 1, 1825.
Sons-in-law: Ezra Marble, James King, Ebenezer Snow, Jo-
seph Brooks, to have $1. each. Rest of estate to son,
Stephen L. Smith. Exrs. son Stephen, Ezra Marble.
Wit: William Bridgers, R.R.Sharkey, J.H.Pigg.

BOOTHE, CHARLES.

March 12, 1822.
Children: Horace Montreville Boothe and Jeremiah James
Boothe. Mother: mentioned, but not named.
Exrs: John Boothe (brother) and Austin Leake (friend).

FAULKE, ORRAN.

October 26, 1820.
Brothers: Alfred Faulk and Wilson Faulk.
1/3 of estate to 5 sisters and one half sister, lately
married. "I wish my father, William Faulk, to be sup-
ported." Exrs: brothers Alfred and Wilson Faulk.

MARRIAGES

Arthur, Isham	-- Mary Wiseman, Sept. 1, 1819.
Alford, Jesse	-- Peggy Fife, July, 8, 1817
Anderson, William	Sarah Surgant, ------

"B"

Beard, Joseph	- Sally Weeks
Blanton, Benjamin	- Narcissa Watson, Oct.5, 1816
Bool, Bernhart	- Elizabeth Fowler, June 22, 1817
Bains, Abraham	- Anna M. Willis, Nov. 27, 1817
Beard, George	- Catherine Ivers, Jan.6,1818
Beiller, Joseph	- Margaret Mackey, March 16, 1818
Bridges, Elias	- Tennessee Janehill,Nov.17, 1818
Ballow, Jonathan	- Mary Jones -----.
Barbridge, Robert	- Eliza A. Barnes, Sep.22, 1819
Bradford, Murphy	- Priscilla Anderson, April 21'19
Ballow, Leonard	- Eliz. Moore, April 8, 1819
Bruce, Benjamin	- Rachel P. Puckett, May 20, 1820
Bradford, M.James	- Ann E. Barnes, July 3, 1820
Brashears, Tobias	- Matilda Duncan, July 28, 1820
Burbridge, Joseph	- Philena Newman, Sep.6, 1817
Bailey, Joseph	- Margaret Mackey, March 16,1818
Booker, William	- Susan Calhoun, Sept.3C, 1816
Bolls, John	- Mary Lobdell, Feb.8, 1819
Buchanan, John	- Sarah Henning, Oct.15, 1816
Beasly, William	- Rebecca Foster, April 24'20

"C"

Cook, Edward	- Celia White, Aug.1, 1817
Cummins, Wilson	- Jane Conger----
Conger, William	- Rachel Thompson, Aug. 3, 1817
Cook, John	- Mary Williams, Aug.14, 1816
Cunningham, John	- Gincy McDonald, Sep. 30, 1816
Coe, Thomas	- Jane Glascock, Aug.30, 1818
Corbet, Abel	- Nancy Truit, July 13, 1818
Clark, Lewis, Jr.	- Polly Stilly, July 14, 1818
Cooper, William	- Margaret Wright, Feb.21, 1819
Cameron, John	- Demarias Taylor, Nov. 6, 1819
Chambliss, William R.	- Rebecca Gibson, Nov.17, 1818

"D"

Disharoon, Leven	- Elizabeth Harlley, Feb.10,1817
Drewer, Christopher	- Rosa Herring, March 14, 1817
Dorsey, Richard	- Phebe Armstrong, April 26, 1818
Davis, Samuel	- Sarah M. Davis, July 2?, 1818
Dawson, Thomas	- Patsy Brooks, Oct. 6, 1818
Daniel, William	- Elizabeth Taylor, May 1, 1819

Downing, David D.   - Esther Barnes, Dec.30, 1819
Dillingham, L.D.Alfred   - Nancy Thompson, June 20, 1820
Dozer, Timothy   - Hannah Weeks, 18 March, 1819

"E"

Eastly, Andrew   - Nancy Reeves, Sept. 3, 1818

"F"

Foster, Shadrock   - Milly Cox, June 25, 1817
Fisher, George   - Eliza Davis, Oct. 8, 1818
Fife, John M.   - Emily Brocus, Jan. 6, 1820
Fairchild John T.   - Sarah Morrison, May 20, 1820

"G"

Graves, Moses   - Rachel Cogan, April 6, 1817
Grisom, John   - Margaret Briscoe, Dec.13, 1817
Gibson, John   - Martha Lindsay, March 24, 1820
Going, Thomas   - Sally Allen, Feb.9, 1820
Grace, John   - Cath. Winterbowers, May 9,1819
Gee, Sack P.   - Mary Ann Brook, May 21, 1820
Griscom, John   - Elizabeth Walker, June 3, 1819
Gibson, David   - Mary Mundell, May 1, 1820
Green, William M.   - Lama McCaleb, August 10, 1818

"H"

Humphrey, George David   - Mary Coburn, Dec. 20, 1816
Hall, John   - Peggy Jones, Sept. 2, 1816
Hudnell, Josiah   - Levina Aarons, Jan.5, 1818
Hall, James   - Vashie D. Smith, Feb.8, 1820
Hopper, George   - Cynthia Leggett, July 27, 1820
Hamilton, Cyrus   - Margaret Wile------

"J"

Jenkins, William   - Polly Murphy, May 10, 1817
Jingles or Ingles, Thomas - Polly Barnes, July 23, 1818
Johnston, Jesse   - Mary McAllister, Sept. 20, '18
Johnston, William   - Eliza Sargent, ----
Jones, Dudley   - Susan Hubbard ----
Johnson, Edward   - Esther Leggett, Feb.3, 1820
John, Edward, Jr.   - Juda Liggett, May 29, 1819
Jeffers, Osborne   - Jane-------- Jan.23, 1819
Johnston, Thomas   - Elizabeth Purvis, Feb. 26, 1818
Jones, David   - Nancy Reeves, May 27, 1818
Jordan, James M.   - Elizabeth Fitzgerald, Sep.5'17

"L"

Lang, John   - Lucinda Reynolds, July 11, 1818

Linning, Joel - Anna Smith, March 23, 1819
Lobdell, Abraham - Malindor Mullin, Oct. 30 '19
Lambly, Turner - Katherine Hainman -------

"M"

McKee, James - Mary McKee, Aug.14, 1816
McNeil, Hector - Lucy Crane, March 27, 1817
Marshall, Reuben - Rachel Eastman, Sept.2, 1816
Moore, John - Peggy Banks, Oct.20, 1817
McGee, Thomas - Mary Fisher, May 13, 1818
Moore, Joseph - Elizabeth Barnes, Jan. 20, 1818
Mathews, Joseph - Sarah Culbertson, Oct.18, 1817
Mullins, Thomas - Rebecca Brown, Aug. 5, 1818
McLelland, Jesse - Rather Cotten, April 1, 1819
Moore, James - Barbara Week, Dec.9, 1816
Mitchell, Bluford - Sally Evans, Dec.4, 1819
McDonald, Benjamin G. - James (?) Johnston, Sept., 1817

"P"

Powell, Joseph - Phebe White
Phillips, L. Isaac - Louis(?) Eastis, Feb.17, 1819
Phillips, Alfred - Franky Eastis, Feb.17, 1819
Price, Marlin - Phebe Stansberry, 8 Dec. 1818
Pitman, Julius - Sarah Wood, 12 Sept. 1817
Parmel, Joseph - Lydia McGinty, -------
Powers, B. - Mary Moore, 29 Oct. 1816

"R"

Ray, William - Mary McAlpen, 2Aug. 1817
Right, Jesse - Lucy Clark, 17 July, 1817
Ray, Green Valentine - Polly Dee, July 23, 1818
Roberts, M. James - Margt. Green, 16 May, 1818
Ragsdale, Elisha - Elizabeth Throckmorton,
 July 19, 1818
Runsdell, Ezra - Martha Griffin, 27 Jan.1818
Rush, Joseph - Patsy Simmons, 30 Dec. 1817
Ring, Mark - Deborah Duncan, 24 Jan.1820
Ragsdale, Benjamin - Matilda Paul, 18 Nov.1819
Runsdell, Seth - Harriet Mason, 31 March, '19
Runder, John - Nancy Griffin, 28 Nov.1819

"S"

Shafer, Abraham - Elizabeth Humphrey, 13 May,'17.
Smith, Samuel - Mary Osborne, May 1, 1817
Sanders, George - Huldah Armstrong, 30 Jan.'17
Stewart, Charles - Nancy Going, 14 Feb.1818
Sims, Arthur B. - Phebe Conger, 14 Jan. 1819
Smith, William - Nancy Johnson, 15 May,1820
Saxon, Samuel - Milly Ingram, April 8, 1816

"T"

Tharp, Zaccheus	- Luraney Mullins, 24 Feb.1819
Trimmer, Joseph	- Susan McClure ------
Thompson, Robert	- Rebecca Jones, 19 Jan.1820
Temple, Loyd	- Mary Sones (?), 5 May, 1816
Taunchie, George	- Nancy Brice, 4 Nov., 1816

"V"

Vanhorn, James   - Pamelia Hutchimson, 16 June, '19

From Claiborne County Marriage Book "A" August, 1816-1820.

Alvis, Joseph	Mary Flower
Arthurs, George	Nancy Reese
Applegate,	Eliza Dorsey
Alexander, Davis	Mary Eldridge

"B"

Boothe, Charles	Elizabeth Ragsdale
Baldwin, Mordecai	Sarah Gregg
Baker, John	Mary Faught
Bacon, John	Catherine Gormley
Berry, William	Parthenia Hambleton
Boyes, James	Mary Armstrong
Burrell, Nathaniel	Rutha Guinn
Bettis, Julius	Susan Clark
Burns, John	Christiana Hartley
Bartholomew, Willis	Elizabeth Stampley
Barnes, John	Harriett Willis
Boothe, Joshia	Elizabeth Rhodes
Bentley, Samuel	Ann Lyming
Bradford, Murphy	Cllary Johnston
Burns, Robert R.	Martha A. McCaleb
Berry Thomas Y.	Leinyah Gilbert
Brent, John	Harriett Shaw
Baldwin, Loring H.	Caroline Foster
Buchan, Peter	Sarah Sanders
Benjamin, Eliel	Esther Hanna
Brashears, Tobias E.	Martha Ann Sharp
Bridgers, Abraham B.	Margaret Humphreys
Burton, Lewis	Duliann Elliott
Beale, William	Mary Sidden
Burns, Dennis	Frances Mundell
Brarleton, Edward W.	Teresa Adams
Berry, Thomas	Sarah Gaton
Barnes, Edward F.	Catherine Cop
Bennison, William	Frances Calvit
Booth, John	Sarah Prior
Baldwin, Mordecai	Lucy Arthur
Barnes, George	Elizabeth Cooper
Barnes, John A.	Sarah Humphreys
Bradlove, A.W.	Susan J. Clarke
Burns, John	Elizabeth Lyon
Beard, Samuel	Ophelia Bullock
Briscoe, William	Elizabeth Scott.

"C"

Clingan, George W	Charity Dillard
Codwise, William F.	Margaret L.E.Campbell
Cleveland, William	Nancy Parker
Camp, Iepe	Nancy Cox
Cotton, Joab	Mahala Dowse
Cotton, John E.E.	Abigail Herring
Caudle, David	Nancy Willett
Cummings, John R.	Elizabeth Wood
Criswell, Robert A.	Sophia Lyons
Carpenter, L.C.	Charlotte Tamer
Cooper, Solomon	Mary Cooper
Chisholm, W.A.A.	Pomina Dillard
Cummings, Tobias	Phebe Flower
Cohee, David P.	Nancy Corbet
Clenmy, Jehn(?)	Julia Ann Taylor
Clarke, Peter N.	Lydia Clemens
Coleman, Pepe (Jesse?)	Sarah Mackey
Coursey, John	Elizabeth Bland
Coleman, Michael	Polly Parish
Calvit, John	Margaret Six
Cook, James E.	Cintha Hutchins
Cook, Benjamin C.	Sophia W. Wiseman
Crowley, Louis	Louisa White
Christian, Nicholas H.	Amanda Norrell
Coe, Francis P.	Amanda Norrell
Campbell, R.W.	H.C. Breazeale
Cammack, Yelverton	E.H. Watson
Couch, James	Polly Dees
Clarke, William	Thena A. Philips
Callender, Joseph	S.W.Breazeale
Clark, Orange	Catherine Quinn

"D"

Dunagan, John T.	Mary Robin
Dean, John R.	Hetty Boothe
Douglas, James	Martha Evans
Dotson, William	Mary Jane Bryce
Dorsey, Bates	Nancy Sargent
Dart, Christopher	Elizabeth Price
Douglas, James S.	Emeline Evans
Denton, Solomon G.	Fanny Alford
Dean, Jese	Dorsia Maybias
Dorsey John P.	Ann E. Hoit
Daniel, Archibald	Catherine Beard
Daniell, Smith C.	Priscilla Skinner
Dilliard, Allen B.	Elizabeth Flowers
Denny, William H.D.	Louise Rouse
Davenport, David	Hetty Miller
Davis, John	Frances Twiner
Downs, Alfred C.	Mary I. Robinson

"E"

Elliott, Middleton	Tabitha Burton
Eastman, David A.	Charlotte Rundell
Evans, George W.	Rachel Phillips
Edwards, Charles H.	Sarah Stanard
Edmunds, H.C.	Lenora Shillings
Edwards, Samuel	Mariah Hane McCreery

"F"

Frizell, William	Racheil Morrison
Foster, Hugh	Winny Arnold
Fife, William	Ann Purvis
Freeman, Isaac	Charlotte Seviere
Fraker, Thompson	Feerby Hall
Faulk, Alfred	Indiana White
Faith, Archibald,	Nancy Newman
Faught, John	Susan Brock
Flemming, E.A.	Ruth Dunham

"G"

Goza, John	Alvah Lum
Gayton, John	Letty Brown
Gibsoh, David D.	Katherine Knowland
Green, Filmer W.	Emily H. McCaleb
Gancy, John	Rachel Long
Gilbert, Gustavus	Elizabeth Rawls
Green, Abraham	Ann B. Maxwell
Gower, Thomas J.	Martha H. Bevol
Goza, Francis F.	Isabella Harvey
Griffith, Evan	Martha Dale
Goodwin, William	Delia Foster
Goodail, James	Sarah Shuffield
Gibson, Thomas J.	Ann Gibson
Goza, Elijah	W.C. Elliott
Goodwin, Samuel	Cynthia Kitchens
Goff, William B.	Leurana Heill
Grafton, James	Maria Heill

"H"

Harmon, Joseph	Eliza H. Sims
Haring, Cornelius	Mary E. Hughes
Hartley, John	Hariet Sharkey
Hamberlin, Anthony	Frances Marble
Hay, John	Ruth Dees
Holland, George	Martha M. Maxey
Hutchinson, James A.	Catherine Bryce
Harris, George	Mary Cooper
Hall, Samuel	Cynthia Hall
Hughes, Preston	Elizabeth Grear
Herring, Edward	Jane Lemmons

"I"

Impson, Benjamin	Martha Adir
Isget, William	Sarah Dunham

"J"

Jones, William	Sarah Simpson
Johnston, Joseph	Nancy Grubbs
Jones, Jesse	Sarah Gibson
Jourdan, Thomas	Catherine Mackey
Johnston, Gideon	Beaulah Gilbert
James, James	Anna Moore
Johnson, Edward	Sarah Sharp
James, Benjamin	Sarah Lilley
Jouncton, John G.	Phebe Goodwin
Jaques, George F.	Charlotte Copland
Jones, Milton	Kezia Culverson
Jrion, Robert A.	Ann A. Dick
Jennison John R.	Catherine Puckett
Jones, Druny	Catherine Fisher
Jones, Mones	Levina White

"K"

Kelly, William	Margaret Cooper
Kevin, Garrett	Lucy Leake
King, John S.	Huldah Flowers
Kirkwood, Robert	Mary Glass
Kelly, Hiram	T.E.Bruce

"L"

Legitte, John T.	Easther Culbertson
Lows, John	Eda Rushion
Lake, George	Malinda Ann McCaleb
Lumley, Turner	Ann Foster
Legitt, Wright	Amanda Flowers
Lum, Israel	Elizabeth Smith
Lane, William B.	Ann M. Ruth
Luster, Miles	Mary Norrell
Leman, Malcolm	Mary Wingfield
Lundegren, Daniel	Nancy Brock
Lyle, William	Lavina Robertson
Long, Charles	Susan Harrell
Lum, Isarel	Matilda Caroline Duval
Lum, William	Clarke Ann Givson
Lowes, Francis	Rodia Rushen
Lowes, Robert	Sarah Johnston
Lovejoy, Jon L.	Phebe Arons
Luckett, James,	Amelia A. Mathews
Legitt, John F.	Phebe Rundell
Lacy, John O.	Mary Ann Danover
Legitt, William	Lavina Sharp

"M"

Murphy, Andrew W.	Sophia E. Ale
Moore William	Anna Bowman
Matthews, Samuel J.	Matilda Norrell
Murphy, William	Lidea Gonshiear
Moore, John	Mary M. Iagua
Magruder, Thomas B.	Elizabeth Harrington
Morrison, Joseph T.	Mary Davenport
Murphy, Vincent	Susan Watson
Mansfield, Nathan	Lucinda Marvin
Mays, Elijah W.	Caroline Montgomery
Moore, Thomas	Permelia Quinn
Masey, Drewer	Sally Gull
Marler, George	Nancy Powell
Mays, George A.	Mary A. Montgomery
Moore, Joseph	Jane Gable
Morten, Jesse	Elizabeth Bentley
Miller, John S.	Martha Middleton
Morris, Lewis C.	Ann E. Daniell
Mitchell, John J.	Harriett Mitchell
Moore, James	Polly J. Perkins
Metcalf, Albert G.	Eveline McCalob
Middleton, Gadi	Susan Ann Lackey
McAlpine, Duncan	Catherine Harvey
McAlpine, Malcom	Mary Johnson
McClure, James	Tabathy Lilly
McClure, William	Sarah Goza
McGohan, Peter	Nancy Justice
McIntyre, Angus	Elizabeth Stilley
McAlpine, John	Margaret Harvey
McEvers, Archibald	Catherine Alford
McAlpine, William R.	Melvina Harris
McIntyre, William	Hanney Carman
McGabb, Edward	Mary E. Wornell

"N"

Nielions, Andrew	Mary Brown
Nugent, Percy	Louisa Doney
Neele, Robert	Ann Rains
Nin, James	Eleanor Buckley
Neill, William	Eliza Brinson
Neele, Thomas S.	Rebecca Roblin
Newell, Thomas M.	Martha Ann Henderson
O'Neill, Tarry	Lucinda Howell

"O"

Ogden, Henry	Nancy Johnson

"P"

Parks, John C.	Margaret Allen
Powell, Lewis	Elizabeth Sheffield

94

Price, Ralph	Clarissa Wilkinson
Patton, William	Elizabeth Wilkinson
Powell, John	Betsy Arinton
Puckett, Douglas C.	Elizabeth Duval
Patrick, Wilder J.	Mary Ballow
Powell, Lewis	Filena Brooks
Putnam, A.W.	Catherine A. Savier (Seveir)
Powell, Samuel R.	Mahala Rogers
Pucket, James D.	Jane Martial
Parlin, Elijah	Betsy Richards
Puckett, William H.	Piaty Clarke

"R"

Ross, Junior	Sarah Elliotte
Roberts, David	Nancy Sharp
Rohelia, Emmanuel	Elizabeth Tanchill
Robinson, Augustus W.	Judith Amanda Truly
Roberts, Paul	Peggy Jones
Richards, Thomas	Rebecca Reeves
Roan, Eliphalet	Polly Gibson
Roberts, John	Elizabeth Roland
Randell, Amor	Sidney Levias
Randolph, Thomas	Clarissa Robins
Robinson, James	Leah Fooks
Rushing, John	Lucinda Hutchinson
Ritchie, Charles	Elizabeth Dale
Robertson, Robert	Sarah Jones
Ragsdale, John M.	Sarah Cooper
Ridge, James	Ruth Sidden
Rundell, Lewis	Salome Eastman
Reynolds, John H.	Martha Coleman
Roberts, John M.	Caroline Stampley
Richlow, Samuel I.	Florena H. McFater

"S"

Sanders, Robert	Ann Gibson
Simmons, Thomas	Martha Allison
Sugg, William	Margaret Daniel
Stanfield, James	Elizabeth Weeks
Stone, Thomas	Amelia Watkins
Stampley, Jacob	Mary Flower
Stowers, James	Margaret McAllister
Scarborough, Patrick R.	Mercy Alvis
Strong, Richard	Ellen Bray
Shields, Benjamin	Susah Desham Chum
Scott, James	Martha James
Spencer Peleg	Elizabeth Moore
Stephens, Isaac	Elizabeth Ragsdale
Stafford, Daniel	Catherine McAllister
Smith, Ebe	Penelope Lewis
Shields, Benjamin	Cassandra Chum
Sharp, Thomas	Elizabeth Shilling

Snodgrass, John	Margaret Price
Strother, Thompson	Elizabeth Marble
Smith, Stephen L.	Drucilla Marble
Sidden, James D.	Fanny Morris
Strother, Walter	Harriet Hartley
Spears, William	Thersea Ann Shillings
Stowers, Caleb	Frances Tutt
Stampley, Richard	Abigail Smith

"T"

Tabor, William	Ann Brashears
Trewit, William	Elizabeth Powell
Taull, Elbrige	Mary Crockett
Taylor, John P.	Mary Daniel
Turner, Samuel	Elizabeth Briscoe
Truly, Bennett R.	Eliza H. Ussery
Thompson, William	Hannah Ballow
Tharp, Nathan	Margaret McRoy
Turners, Sugars	Susan Barnes
Thompson, Jene	Emily Bullock
Taylor, John E.	Nancy Rains
Tillman, Alfred	Candes Mitchell
Twiner, George	Mary Lemmons
Tidwell, Gideon Q.	Elizabeth C. Neill
Tharp, James	Elizabeth Johnston

"V"

Venables, John	Elizabeth Sims
Vanse, Samuel P.	Tamsey Tiltotson
Vanhorn, James	Lucinda Abbey
Vories, James M.	Elizabeth Strauss
Valentine, John	Elizabeth Roberts
Vandorn, P.A.	Sophia Caffery

"W"

Weatherington, Gabriel	Sarah Cooper
White, William	Elizabeth Baker
Walker, William	Mary Rundell
Woodward, Thomas	Sally Armstrong
White, Henry M.	Phebe White
White, Richard	Martha White
White, Thompson	Susan Herring
Whiting, Amos	Maria Louisa Lansdale
Walton, Ira	Jane Bland
White, William	Philena Marble
Watson, James, Jr.	Melinda Crane
Watkins, Josiah L.	Sally Evans
White, James D.	Mary Blackwell
Washburn, William	Elizabeth Bowls
Weems, Hardy	Rachel Craig
White, John D.	Sally Aarons

Watkins, William	Sarah Daniels
Wood, Agulla (Aquilla)	Nancy Camp
Wallace, George T.	Winny Barfield
Wheeler, George	Hannah Ferguson
Willis, Daniel	Elizabeth Copland
Watson, Ivy H.	Sally Barnes
Wilson, William	Rosannah Long
Whits, William	Mary Bullard
Walker, Henry D.	Mary Miller
Watson, Jeremiah	Frances Lowry
Wallace, J.W.E.	Harriett Hoit
Watkins, Benjamin	Elenor Patton
Warren, B. Jeremiah	Elizabeth Briscoe
Wheeles, Greenbury	Martha Culbertson
Watson, Meredith	Juliana Clenny

"Y"

Young, William	Clarissa Christy (Christie)
Yates, Ignatus	Obedience Arthur.

Arthur, Isham
Armstrong, A. (Estate)
Armstrong, Alexander, Jr.
Arnold, William M.
Armstong, J.M.
Applegate, J.P.
Alexander, G.A.
Abrams, H.W.
Arnolds Petty & Co.
Anketell, John
Alexander, John
Alexander, Robert
Adams, James
Anderson, H. & H.O.
Ancher, James (Estate)
Allso, Gideon
Adere, Isaac (estate)
Allison, James
Armitage, J.
Abby, S.F.R.
Anderson, James
Applegate, Robert

Briscoe, E.C.
Buck, William
Barnes, Elias
Brock, Joseph F.
Berry, Thomas
Brinson, Gance (Estate)
Brinson, George
Buckhannan, John (Estate)
Booth, John
Booth, Charles (Estate)
Butler, N.W.
Bruce, Madison
Brenton, J.E.C. (Estate)
Bruce, Uriah
Ballard & Walters
Ballard & Sullivan
L.W. Ballard
Bingham, Thomas & Co.
Bridewell, William &Co.
Bobo, Abraham (Estate)
Bridgers, Abram
Bush, William D.
Breashears, T.E.
Burns, Dennis

Brown & Fisher
Brown, Chas. (Estate)
Buckler, Daniel
Buckler, Allen
Barnes, Mary
Bridgers, A.B.
Breashears, Eden
Benton, John W.
Bridgers, William
Beathea, Redwick
Bobbett, Green
Britt, John
Brown, Henry
Bridgers, Elias
Brown, John
Bearbower, William
Bridewell, William
Boardman, Daniel
Bryant, Thomas
Burbank, Chas.S.
Broashear, F.B. (Estate)
Boyd, James
Bell, Isaiah (colored)
Bell, Henry (colored)
Bell (Andrew (colored)
Breazeale, Mary
Breazeale, D.W. (Estate)
Bentley, Samuel A.
Barnes, Abraham (Estate)
Barnes, Catherine
Ballenger, Jesse
Bird, William
Brazelton, E.W.
Burnes, James
Bolls, Matthew
Briscoe, William
Briscoe, Thomas (Estate)
Briscoe, Philip
Briscoe, Andrew
Bradshaw, Sarah
Bradshaw, James
Bradshaw, L.
Bane, G.H.
Bland, R.J.
Benton, J.H.
Bridewell, John L.
Buck, John L.
Bridgers, Samson

Barnes, John
Brown, Robert P.
Bryant, Benjamin
Bloodworth, Thomas
Brandon, Samuel
Black, William
Beale, William
Boaty, William
Benton, Bryan
Bolls, Lewis
Burnet, John
Bonner, Jane
Buchanan, Walter
Bullard, Joseph
Breazeale, Willis (Estate)
Burrough, Josiah
Butler, Zebulon
Barland, James
Briscoe, P.
Bullock, Mary (Estate)
Burnes, Emaley
Biggs, A.
Bell, Col. Hiram
Bank, Planters Branch
Breshears, M.F. (Estate)
Bull, William
Brown, F.S.
Booth, Hester
Berry, Thomas
Baldwin, M.
Bridgers, John D.
Bridgers, Joseph
Barefield, Richard

Clark, William
Cox, Samuel
Clark, Orange
Clark, George S.
Coleman, William
Carr, James
Chunn, Nahum
Coe, Thomas
Clark, Robert
Choat, A.H.
Cook, Thomas
Cox, Moses
Collin, Frederick
Cooper, Benjamin
Cooper, James
Cotter, Thomas
Callinder, Joseph

Compton, W.S.
Cook, Samuel
Cronly, Louis
Carpenter, H. & Co.
Cocks, L.
Coleman, William
Cocks, H.
Coapland, Mary
Colson, Jacob
Colley, Richard
Cartmill, H.
Currie, R.M.
Collins, James
Cathcart, H.W.
Calhoun, P.C.
Castleman & Rogers
Choat, Isaac
Coleman, Jeremiah
Chaivous, Jourdan
Calvit, John
Calvit, James
Cobun, L. & J.B.
Coleman, Jeremiah
Cotter, James
Coleman, Asa
Cumpton, William
Cobun, Ann
Cooper, Cannon W.
Connor, W.H.
Carodine, Richard
Carodine, John
Cogan, F.W. (Estate)
Crane, James
Cox, Robert
Cox, William
Cox, F.J.
Cox, John, David and George
Cox, Josiah
Chamberlain, Jeremiah
Chamberlain, John
Crow, John
Crow, Clark
Coleman, Israel
Coleman, Elijah
Cook, David
Campbell, R.W.
Chaplain, W.R.F.
Clark, E. (Estate)
Chevenderman, A.
Christie, William (Estate)
Caison, Charles
Clark, Alfred

Cobun, William
Clarke, E.L., Sr.
Clarke, Gibson & Chas.B.
Clarke, E.L, Jr.
Chess, A.
Creighton, Fletcher
Cooper, William W.
Cook, Stephen
Cissna, William W.
Couch, James
Carraway, J.S & L.
Carraway, Thomas
Carpenter, H. & Co.
Cooper, Mahban
Cooper, Harrison, Sr.
Cooper, Harrison, Jr.
Cooper, John
Cooper, William Claiborne
Coffey, Caskey
Conger, John B.
Chamberlain, James
Carson, Francis
Cheatham, F.R.
Carroll, William
Creigh, Henry (Heirs)
Carson, Stephen (Estate)
Chambliss, R. (Estate)
Clarke, M. & G.W. Reynolds
Cochran, Robert
Chambliss, Ann

Dorsey, Samuel
Dorsey, Edward
Dilliam, W.F.
Derrah, James
Dickson, Amos
Duvall, Lewis
Dee Woods & Co.
Dunoughn, D.O.
Davenport, David
Davis, Hervey
Dale, John H.
Darnall, John
Davenport, Joseph
Davenport, James
Downing, D.D. (Estate)
Davenport, Ephiram
Davenport, Isaac (Estate)
Daniell, Smith C.
Davis, David (Estate)
Davis, Thomas
Dorsey, Bates
Donny, William, H.D.
Duncan, Berry (c)

Davis, William
Davis, R. (Estate)
Dean, John R.
Darden, Elizabeth
Daniel, William
Dorsey, William & Owing
Davis, James
Delaughters, James
Delaughters, Tilman
Dillard, Wiley
Dameron, Jemina (Estate)
Dickerson, W.C.
Drake, A.R.
Daughtery, Joseph
Defrance, M.F. (Estate)
Daniel, Josiah J. (Estate)
Dunkerson, Thomas
Davis, Joseph E.
Douglas, James S.
Douglas, A. (Estate)
Dethroge, Zeland (Estate)
Delaughter, Thomas
Dunn, Abijah

Eagin, G.
Ewing, Willis
Elder, James
Ewing, John
Eskridge & Furinquent (?)
Eskridge, L. P.
Evan, Joseph
Evan, Lewis (Estate)
Elmore, Joseph
Elmore, Elijah
Elmore, Levi
Erwin, William (Estate)
Eddins F.
Eddins, G.W.
Eddins, Abrams
Elliott, Uriah
Edwards, Jonathan
Evans, F.J.
Egan, D.B.
Evans, E. (Estate)
Evans, George
Elliott, William & George
Eastman, Levi
Eastman, Caroline

Frisby, Daniel
Fife, Gilbert
Fife, William
Fife, John M.
Fanchild, J.B. & Co.
Fisher, John

Humphrey, G.D.
Humphrey, D.S.
Humphrey, G.W.
Heath, A.
Hall, Solomon,
Hill, Martha
Hill, E.B.
Hooper, A.A.
Hooper, John
Hamilton, Charles
Hamilton, Richard
Hunter, Milford
Humphrey, B.G.
Hogan, J.L.
Hedden, Ira J.
Henry, John (Col.)
Holderman, B.
Hall, Richard
Hays, John
Holley, Christopher (Col.)
Harris, Hardeman (Col.)
Harris, Turner
Hubbard, Cock
Harris, James
Hieker, J.W.
Herlbert, Benoi
Hall, James
Hunt, Daniel (Estate)
Hughes, Henry
Harris, George
Hodge, A.W.
Hamilton, R.S.
Hendebert (?), James
Henderson, William (Estate)
Hall, E.
Harring, E.W.
Hester, Isaiah
Harmon, John
Hutchins, James
Hutchins, Felemicus
Hasting, William
Harmon, Stephen
Herren, Richard
Heuston, Abram
Hedrick, John (Heirs)
Hedrick, G.C.
Hale, Charlotte
Hooper, Passemore
Hughes, B.
Hoyt, George
Herrell, Benjamin
Hutchinson, L.C.
Hall, L.F.B.

Hunt, A.D.
Harmon, Joseph
Harmon, Hezekiah (Estate)
Howard, Thomas
Henderson, John
Hughes, P.A.
Hunt, Abijah
Hooper, D.H.
Harring, Aaron (Estate)

Ingram, A.
Ingram, Mary
Ingles, William

Jones, William
Jones, George (Estate)
Jones, David
Jones, Jonathan
Jones, George W.
Jones, Thomas
Jones, James
Johnston, John
Jacques, Charlotte
Jennings, John (Estate)
Johnston, John W.
Jacob, Elias
Jobe, Robert B.
James, E.H.
Jefferee, Curtis
Jones, Joseph E.
Jones, James W.
Jones, R.B.
Jefferee, Thomas D.
Jefferee, Sydney
Jones, F.G.
Johnston, Thomas
Jones, Z.B. (Estate)
Johnston, John T.
Jefferee, E.S.
Jones, Wiley (Estate)
Jones, John

Kelly, Hiram
Kemball, James
Knight, Robert
King, William
Kitchens, Josiah
Killians, George
King, James W.
Kinley, David
Kinley, J.H.
Kippell, G.H.
King, William

Kinnison, William	Miller, Benjamin
Kennedy, Robert	Maury, I.H.
King, A.W.	Marble, Ezra
Kilerase, William	McBeth, James
Knowlton, John	McDougal, Daniel
King, Prosper	Moore, James
Kea, Wiley	Marble, Stephem
	Marble, Desiah (Estate)
Longina, F.	McMahara, John
Lovelace, G.L.	Malone, C.
Longhorn, John (Estate)	Mathew, W.E.
Lake, George	Morris, E.
Levey, Lewis	Maddox, A.B.
Luster, Miles	Morris, Lewis C.
Lunn, Isarel	Montgomery, Robert
Leadbetter, Sneld	Marlin, F.R.
Lyle, William	McIntire, F.G.
Lynn, Margaret	Mason, C.
Lecount, S.	McDonald, Daniel
Livingston, Samuel	McElwoe, Stephen (Heirs)
Livingston, Isaac	Moore, Joseph (Estate)
Lemmans, Gilbert	McGill, James (Estate)
Leak, Nichols	McCall, Dougall
Logan, Margaret	Murdock, John (Estate)
Logan, William	Mitchell, John J.
Luckett, James	Mitchell, Edward
Long, John	Mitchell, Joab
Lowes, John	Mitchell, Jesse
Lee, Edward	Mitchell, Benjamin
Lackey, William	Metcalf, H.
Leroux, Lewis (Estate)	Montgomery, Alexander
Lyons, Peter	McLeod, Alexander
Leggett, Samuel	McCroson, Gilbert
Loring, Isarel	McFeeters, Theophilus
Luster, George	McMear, David
Lemmons, John	McAn, Samuel B.
Ludlow, A.B.	Moore, Allen
Lemmons, Williams	McVoy, Joseph
Lee, Charles	Montgomery, G.W. & Mary Ann
Lee, David	McAnnly, B.S.
	Murphy, A.W.
Moore, Robert F.	McCalibb, Jonathan
Magruder, F.B.	McCalibb, David
Moore, Col. Dood	Miller, A.H.
Murdock, Francis	McNeill, John and James
McCoy, Robert	McFolters, Alexander
McClure, James, Jr.	McIntire, Samuel
McClure, James, Sr.	McNall, James
McIntire, Peter	McNall, William
McIllhany, John M.	Moore, James B.
Muncaster, C.W.	Minor, Stephen (Heirs)
Muncaster, E.A.	Moore, James
Mullins, D.C.	Moore, John (Estate)
Martin, Alexander	Maxwell, James A.
Mears, William D.	Moore, Thomas

Miller, Margaret
Miller, Joseph
McClauslin, William
Mitchell, Polly
McGelvary, Alexander
McKee, Coapland
Moore, Calvin
Martin, William
Marlin, William H.
Mead- Coles
Marshall, William

Neeley, Sydney
Neeley, William W.
Neill, William
Neill, John
Norman, James
Novel, John
Nobbs, Virgin
Newell, E.D.
Newell, F.M.
Newman, Isaac (Heirs)
Newman, Uriah
Nelson, William
Newman, Joseph H.
Neeley, John G.
Norrell, Levi
Noland, William
Nelson, R.
Nicolls, Joseph
Newman, Reuben
Neeley, Rebecca

Overstreet, Thomas
Ostean, Gabriel
Osburn, James
Owins, Thomas
Owens, William
Ogden, Richard
Offutt-------

Patton, Francis
Powell, I.J.
Patterson, John
Powell, J.M.
Philips, Thomas C.
Philips, Lee M.
Payar, Green
Prince, B.E.
Patton, Robert
Patton, William (Estate)
Puckett, D.C.
Palton, James
Parkes, Thomas
Page, John W.

Powell, Martin
Pope, Henry
Pugh, William
Pate, Joel (Estate)
Pate, A.
Pate, Mary
Page, Isaac
Pugh, John R.
Patterson, D.B.
Parmer, H.F.
Pettit, Alexander
Peers, I.W.
Peers, A.
Powers, E.D.
Petty, P.A.
Patterson, William L.
Patterson, James H.
Price, Ralph
Price, Lewallon
Price, Phil
Payne, P.
Payne, Samuel
Perkins, Isaac
Patton, James
Patton, John
Peck, A.H.
Puckett, William
Powers, Isaac
Price, Joseph
Philip, Joseph
Philip, Alfred
Philip, Isaac
Price, William
Porter, Wesley
Putnam, A.W.
Parker, Isaac
Pope, H.W.
Pitman, O.F.
Pendleton, William W.
Parker, James
Posey, A.
Poindexter, George
Perkins, John
Parker, Josiah

Quinn, Lemuel

Rondell, Seth
Rains, John
Roland, John S.
Rush, Joseph
Rail, John
Reid, Jacob B.
Ragsdale, Francis
Ragsdale, E. (Estate)

Ransdoll, F.P.
Reynolds, Josiah
Rendell, Simon
Richards, John
Robinson, Benjamin (Estate)
Robertson, Joseph
Rusk, William L.
Rogers, I.H.
Ricketts, H.
Roach, James
Robertson, Rederick
Ross, Isaac
Rundill, Daniel
Rundill, Ezra
Rains, Littleton
Rendill, Mary
Roberts, Hiram
Robinson, William G.
Rhodes, Sarah
Rawls, John C.
Reynolds, G.W.
Ragsdale, Lucy
Reagan, R. (Estate)
Richard, Thomas
Ridge, J.
Robinson, Amos
Ricklow, S.I.
Ricklow, E.J.
Ricklow, Jacob
Ross, Isaac, Jr.
Robertson, Thomas W.
Roan, Eliphalet
Ragsdale, John (Estate)
Rogers, John
Reaves, Johnston

Sanders, Robert
Shields, L.M.
Standsborough, Jesse
Shelby, M.D.
Simmons, James
Scott, Robert (Estate)
Scott, W.B.
Scott, Robert
Saxon, Joshua (Estate)
Sherwood, George
Shields, Benjamin
Singleton, John G.
Sheffield, James, John & Mary
Stockton, B.F.
Shaw, Sexton
Spiers, William
Sharkey, R.R.
Simmonds, Thomas
Summers, G.W.

Skinner, John
Smith, G.W.
Spencer, Peleg
Stone, Thomas
Snow, E.
Sugg, Josiah
Sanders, Geo.
Shannon, James
Shoultz, J.D.
Smith, William
Stamps, John
Scofield, G.H.
Stuart, William
Saucer, John
Smith, Lombard
Silver, A.E.
Shoemaker, D.
Snodgrass, John
Stowers, Lewis
Stuart, James G.
Scarborough, James G.
Scarborough, Patrick
Skinner, Add.
Sanders, L.B.(?)
Scott, Thomas B.
Sidebottom, John
Sims, William
Sutton, James
Sandefor----
Spencer, H.M.
Spears, James D.
Strother, Thompson
Shaifer, Henry
Silver, Frank
Shoemaker, Phil
Sullivan, A. (Estate)
Seiver, George
Snow, C.B.
Scott, Gabriel (Estate)

Thompson, E.S.
Turtleout, Joseph
Thompson, S.
Trevilion, F.S.
Trevilion, John
Tamar, Henry
Tichenor, C.C.
Turpine (Turpin ?), White
Turpin, F.W.
Taylor, William
Thompson, James
Thompson, Jeremiah
Torrey, James
Thompson, John (Estate)

Thompson, H.
Tompkins----
Tarpley, A.
Terry, I.D.
Tharp, Nathan
Thomas, Thomas G.
Thomas, Samuel
Turner, Samuel
Thompson, J.W.
Tharrington, Herrod
Trimble, A.G.
Tibbetts, S.M.
Taylor, Sam
Taylor, John
Throckmorton, Lewis
Thrasher, S.B.
Torrey, John L.
Townsley, Robert
Thatcher, John
Torrey, Alexander
Tucker, D.A.
Tarver, John
Talman, E.
Trimble, Robert (Estate)

Underwood, Alfred

Venable, John
Virtue, John D.
Vandine, Michael
Virtue, Daniel
Valentine, Richard
Vandome, P.H.
Valentine, Roswell

White, Thompson
Walker, William
Williams, Lewis
Wilkinson, Abner
Wilkinson, J.M.
Wallace, James
Watson, B.H.
Wilkinson, William (Heirs)
Wood, Robert
Waters A. (Estate)
Walton, Parke (Estate)
Woodward, Thomas
Willoughby, William
Walker, William
Wilson, A.M. (Estate)
Walker, Samuel
Webber, R.B.
Wood Heirs

Willis, Josiah (Estate)
West, B.F.
Wilson, Timothy
Winkler, A.
Willis, Daniel
Walker, George
Walther, J.
Whiting & Egan
White, Isaac
Watt, Hugh
Watson, Isaiah
Watson, A.G.
Wheeler, , G.B.
Wheeler, William
Watson, James W.
Wells, E.W.
Willis, William
Wells, Noel
Watson, A.J.
Wright, James R.
Woods, John
Whitfield, A.
Wade, Eli
Wyche, William A. (Estate)
Washburne, John
Washburne, William
Wilson, R.S.
Wainwright ---

Yates, George W.
Yates, E. (Estate)
Yates, Ignatius
Yirby, Allen

Zill, Jesse

ROBERTS, ALLEN.

May 26, 1832. August Court, 1832.
I give and grant unto Martha Saunders (dau.), negro
George. To son William H. Roberts, negro, Berry.
To son Richard S. Roberts, negro, Worthington.
To son Thomas H. Roberts, slave, Gilbert.
To dau. Frances Ann Roberts, slaves- Chancy and Mary.
To son James S. Roberts, slave- Burrell.
To son Joseph Roberts, slaves, Robin and Violet.
All above slaves to be subject to use and control of my
wife, Elizabeth Roberts, during her lifetime, together
with all household and kitchen furniture.
Exr: Samuel Smith. Wit: John Hume and Samuel Young.

BASKINS, ROBERT.

Sept. 5, 1832. Sept. Court, 1832.
To each one of my children the sum of $120. in such prop-
erty as may be designated by my wife, Polly, to be received as they come of age, except my sons, James and
John, and daughter, Polly, as they have already received
that amount of my estate, when daughter Polly gets one
cow and calf more, that I wish her to have. At the decease
of wife, estate to be divided as to give each of my children an equal part.
Executrix: wife Polly
Wit: William Austin, Green Speight, Thomas Coleman.

ROBERTSON, JOHN.

Died October 5, 1832. Will probated Nov. Court, 1832.
"I give and bequeath unto my brother, Thomas Robertson,
$500., and the residue of my property I give in equal
shares to my legal heirs."
Exrs: James Scott and Thomas Robertson (brother).
Wit: William Snow and S. Tracy.

HARRELL, ISAAC.

Dec. 20, 1832. December Court, 1832.
Of Simpson County, Mississippi.
Wife and Executrix: wife Rebecca Harrell.
Wit: James Powell and John Keen.

NICHOLS, HENRY, SR.

Jan. 4, 1833, May 27, 1833.
Gr.children: Wilford Sims, Martha Ann Sims, Mary Ann
Sims, to ha ve one two year old heifer, each. Rest of
estate to kept until youngest child becomes of age,
except 5 cows and calves to son William. Property to
be divided between heirs, except that property received
by Robert I. Sims and Jacob Lott.
Exrs: William Nichols (son) and Joshua Howard.
Wit: Robert I. Sims and Joshua Howard.

CARRIC, ROBERT.

March 14, 1833.   May Court, 1833.
"To wife, land where I now live (170 acres) and 6 slaves,
stock, horses, hogs and sheep. After decease of wife property to be equally divided among children: Jinnett, Edward, Christian, Elizabeth, David, McRae, John Alexander.
Executrix: wife. Wit: Hugh McCall, John Morrison.

TERRELL, JAMES.

Probated July Court, 1833.
Wife: to have property received from her at marriage.
Son: James, to have 1/4 section of land, on which we
now live. All slaves to be kept on plantation in Hinds
County, until children become of age (children not nam-
ed). Exrs: Montalbert Edwards and Samuel Terrell.
Wit: Michael Schall, Meday Bozeman and James M. Terrell.

CATLETT, ELISHA.

Probated July 3, 1833. Nun-cupative will.
Property to be equally divided between wife and mother.
Exrs: Thacker M. Winters and H.G. Runnells.

HIGGS, ELISHA.

Nov. 25, 1813. Feb. 7, 1814. Of Twiggs Co., Georgia.
Estate to be divided between wife, Polly Higgs, and
children- Patsy, Judith, Angus Baldwin, Thomas Flour-
noy Higgs. Exrs: wife and William Jameson.
Wit: Leabourn Mimmos (Mimmus), Henry Lascon, Abraham
Wood.

SEWELL, JOSHUA.

Sept.8, 1833. September Court, 1833.
Estate to be equally divided between children when they

are twenty-one years of age.
Exrs: William Redwine and Joseph Aubrey.
Wit: Jeremiah Conant and E.P.Strange.

LEA, WILLIAM.

Sept. 3, 1833. September Court, 1833.
Son: William Lea, to have slaves, Moses, Nancy, Burns,
Sam and Moses and the children of Nancy, and money
coming from a note. I appoint my friend, Dr. Edward Carroll, of Liberty, Amite County (Miss.), guardian of my
son William. Wife: Sarah Lea, to have all the right,
claim in trust and demand of every nature, kind and disposition on whatsoever to or ensuing from or out of a
certain tract of land in Warren County (Miss.), the same
having descended to her and Mrs. Emily Lea from their
father, Dennis Griffin, one gold watch, riding horse and
one negro, named Andrew. To Mrs. Caroline Carroll, money
from a judgment on Henry Hurst, in Court of Amite County
(Miss.), also note on John Collins. Balance of estate to
wife, Sarah Lea, and son William. To brother Calvin Lea,
wearing apparel and negro boy. Exr: Calvin Lea.
Wit: John Stewart, Alexander Stewart, James Scott.

BRYAN, JAMES, SR.

July 9, 1833. September Court, 1833.
Estate to wife, Elizabeth Bryan, anything remaining at
her decease to be equally divided among the following
children: Mary Hill, John N. Bryan, Nancy Lord, Henrietta
Carr, reserving a few dollars for my daughter, Eleanor
Worsham. Other sons mentioned were: Thomas, James and
William Bryan. Exr: Thomas Bryan (son).
Wit: James Philips, William Neeley, Joseph H. Mendenhall.

BRYAN, THOMAS.

August 21, 1833. September, 1833.
All property left to wife with which to raise and edu-
cate children.   Exrs: wife, James Philips.
Wit: Ebenezer Hill, T.B.L. Hadley and Edwin R. Isker.

PERRY, JACOB.

August 30, 1833. October, 1833.
All estate to wife, Obedience Perry, who is named as
executrix.   Wit: Jesse Puckett, James L. Stephens.

OWENS, JAMES.

Wife: Lucinda.
Children: Martha, Eliza and William Owens.
All property to be held until son William reaches age
of 21 years, and then slaves to be divided between them.
Exr: Draper R. Porter.
Wit: W. Porter, Jr. and William Redwine.

JELKS, DISCON.

Sept. 27, 1833. October, 1833.
Wife: Sarah, to have $100., negro girl and household
goods. Son: George Wallace Jelks, to have all lands
with plantation and personal property. Dau: Louise Pullin,
to have negro and personal property. Dau: Sarah Jelks, to
have 40 acres and personal property. Gr.son: William Wil-
shire Ray, to have $100., management of grandson to George
Wallace Jelks. Exr: son George W. Jelks.
Wit: Thomas Robertson, M. Anderson, F.H. Jennings.

NICHOLS, SARAH.

October 7, 1833. Nov. 25, 1833.
Widow of Wright Nichols. Gr.son: Drury Brown, to have
1/3 of undivided interest of late husband, Wright Nichols,
estate. Gr.dau: Malonag (?) Chandler. Gr.children: heirs
of John Farqular and his wife Nancy, 1/3 part of above
mentioned estate. Dau: Susan Wells the other 1/3 part of
estate. Exr: Drury I. Brown.
Wit: William Spencer and David Fluker.

CARR, CHARLOTTE.

Oct. 23, 1833. November Court, 1833. Nun-cupative will.
Land in Warren County (Miss.) to be sold and money giv-
en my children (not named).
Wit: Peyton Worthy and Lavina Alfred.

HARRIS, JAMES.

Oct. 4, 1833. Oct. 28, 1833. Nuncupative will.
Henry Flowers is requsted to settle business.
Louisa Jonas is bequeathed $500. Father (not named)
to have remainder of estate. Wit: M. Johnson, Ackriel
Crumpler, Simeon W. Bohannon and Henry Flowers.

JACOBS, WALTER.

Jan. 19, 1833. Jan. 28, 1834.
The following children to have $2. each: Joseph, Mordi-
cai, James, Benjamin, Jane Roberts, Parmelia Roberts,

Sarah Roberts, Elenor Roberts.
Wife: Gracie, to have lands, tenements, stock and fur-
niture. Exr: James Bond. Wit: Jonathan Catchings, L.
P. Scali (?).

CONGER, MARTIN.

Dec. 10, 1833. Rec., 1834.
Wife: Susan, to have land, negroes, personal property.
Children: Asberry Bernard, A.Mary, Athelia, Susan, Mar-
garet and unborn child. Nephew: Jeptha Conger, to have
a horse. Exrs: wife and Eli Garner.
Wit: Pierce L. Redwine, W.H. Lane, William Redwine.

BUCKHOLDE, JOHN G.

Sept. 4, 1830. Sept. 20, 1830.
Wife: Adaline.
Children: Charles, John, Eliza, Martha. Property and
slaves to be kept until eldest child, Charles, arrives
at the age of 21 years.
Exrs: wife, Charles Davis.
Wit: Gab Felder, S. Botters, S.H. Strong

FORT, JACOB.

December 6, 1833. January Court, 1834.
Wife: Cynthia. Children: Mary Cornelia, Copelan,
Martha, Mariah, Edwin, Ruthvin, Jacob Milliard Fort.
Exrs: Josiah Fort (bro., of Maderson Co., Tenn.),
Ethereld Williams (of East Tenn.), Orren Battle (of
Hinds Co.). Wit: Sarah Battle, Ann Ross.

CALDWELL, GEORGE.

Feb. 12, 1834. March, 1834.
Wife: Juliann. Children: William Plouden, George Jeffear-
son, Lovey Elizabeth (3 youngest children).
Sons: John H., to have land and slaves ; Edwin James, land
and slaves; George Jefferson, land and slaves.
Exrs: Elisha Andrews, John H. Caldwell.
Wit: Joshua Howard, William Cabeen, William G. Watson.

STOVALL, JOSIAH.

Nov. 17, 1798. December Court, 1798.
Lincoln County, Georgia. All children not receiving
anything shall be given what wife can spare. Dau: Polly,
to have one negro girl- not to be sold. Lends to wife,
Polly Stovall, tract of land they now live upon and slaves.

Mentions small children, but does not name.
Exrs: wife, sons Drewery and Charles.
Wit: Elisha Holmes, John Main, William Wright, Stephen Stovall.

MCREA, MARGARET.

Nov. 15, 1830. December, 1830.
Of Perry County, Miss. Legatees: William P. McRea (gr.son);
Margaret McRae(gr.dau.); Thomas L. Summerall, to hold in
trust, one negro for dau. Isabel Pitman during her life,
and at her decease to gr.son, Daniel McRea Pitman; gr.dau.
Arabella Holt, to have my horse and gig, feather bed and
furniture; Burrell Pitman, to have $2.; dau. Margaret Sum-
merall, to have residue of household furniture.
Wit: John Black, A.C.Jennings, John C. Cox.

MASSENBERG, BENJAMIN HARRISON.

June 19, 1834. October, 1834.   Of Franklin Co., Ala.
Legatee: Cargill Jones Massenberg (nephew).
Wit: John Meehan.

BRENT, WILLIAM.

August 20, 1834.   Sept. 21, 1834.
Wife: Mary, to have land, slaves personalty.
Daughters: Hannah Neal Brent, Virginia Evelyn Brent,
to have land and slaves. Exrs: wife, William De Mass.
Wit: Philip M. Alston, Adaline Alston, Maria Barton.

PORTER, WILLIAM, SR.

August 23, 1833. October 27, 1834.
Wife: Gracy, to have negro woman, furniture, personalty.
Step-sons: John S., Isaac and William Lawson, a horse,
saddle and bridle, each. Step-daus: Julia Ann Retty (
wife of Blanton Chresley), to have a negro; Mary Ann
Lawson, land, money and cattle.
Wife to be guardian of minor children.
Wit: Samuel Puckett, Thomas Shipp.

HILBOURNE, VAUGHN.

Died Sept. 5, 1834. August 27, 1834.
Legatee: Wynana Van Newman.

MURCHISON, JOHN.

Died in August, 1834. Oct. 28, 1834.
Vincent Murphy to take charge until return of brother,
Simon Murchison, from the north. Sister Sarah to have
home on plantation of brother Simon.
Wit: John F. Watson. A nuncupative will.

YESSER, ELINOR A.

Sept. 14, 1834. Sept. 22, 1834.
Children: Elenor Mankey (dau.), to have negroes, riding
horse, red bed stead, feather bed; Daniel H. Yesser (son)
to have 3 negroes, his fathers picture, silver spoons,
silver ladle, chairs and side board; son Archibald, to
have 2 slaves, pictures, books etc; son George W., 2 slaves.
; son Charles R., 5 slaves; dau. Eliza Yesser, 3 slaves,
mahogany bed stead, feather bed, furniture.
Exr: friend, John B. Fox, to hold in trust 3 slaves for
use of daughter, Mary Strother, to secure certain land for
Mary and Prudence Strother. Gr.daughters: Ellen and Mary
Ellen Manks. Wit: T.B. Kilbourn, William Lee Davidson,
Charles R. Lewis.

JONES, JOHN W.

April 1, 1835.
Wife: Caroline. Children: George, Joseph, Margaret.
Exr: William Lambeth (friend).
Wit: E.D. Fenner, I.B. Morgan, Lewis Bond.

BUGG, NANCY.

April 25, 1831. April 27, 1835.
Legatees: son Benjamin, to have negro woman and boy;
dau. Lucy Kyle and her husband, Claiborne Kyle, to have
negro boy; dau. Mary Young and her husband, Ephiram
Young, to have a negro named Dilcy; dau. Rebecca Young,
personalty; gr.dau. Adeline Young (dau. of Mary and Ephiram Young), side saddle. Exr: son Benjamin.
Wit: Thomas Williams and Daniel Williams.

PURVIS, GILBERT JOHNSON.

April 9, 1835. April 27, 1835.
Property now in controversy with James, P.J., and Will-
iam Purvis, and can make no bequests. Property of late
father, Gilbert Purvis. (Gilbert Johnson Purvis claimed
all property mother possessed at time of her death).
Sister Sally Purvis to have $150. per year.
Exrs: John and William Purvis.
Wit: William H. Young and Charles C. Mayson.

THOMPSON, JENNETT.

April 28, 1834. April, 1835.
Legatees: sister, Mary Mooney, to have one suit of
wearing apparel to be selected by Charlotte F.A.
Thompson; remaining wearing apparel to be divided between daughters, Charlotte Thompson and Sarah Miles;
sons John B. and Thomas G. to have $160. each; gr.son
William F. Farrell, son of Elizabeth Farrell, to have
$100.; gr.children (children of Sarah Miles)- James,
David, Harriett and Eliza Jane Miles, to have money that
is due me from Thomas G. Thompson and Samuel Brown; dau.
Eliza Miles, personalty; son S.G. Thompson, negroes; gr.
dau. Mary Jennett Thompson, dau. of S.G. Thompson, personalty. Exrs: Samuel Brown (brother), Thomas G. Thompson (son). Wit: Stephen Austin, John Sebie, Charles
Horton.

FORTNER, ARTHUR.

Jan. 24, 1835. May 9, 1835.
All estate to wife Martha and daughter Susan.
Exrs: wife, Benjamin Fortner.
Wit: Olne Redwine, John Lee.
(A large estate of land and slaves.)

WELLS, STEPHEN.

May 4, 1835. July, 1835.
To Sally Wells, land, slaves, personalty.
Sons: Stock A. and Stephen Wells, land and slaves.
Daughters: Feeaceah (?) Wells, Eliza Wells and Sarah
Brown. Exrs: sons Miles and William.
Wit: Olin (Olm) Spencer, William C. Spencer, James. L.
Farquhar. Old slave, Esther, to have her freedom and
live with any of my children she desires.

BAILEY, WILLIAM.

Probated Oct. 26, 1835. Probated in Christian Co., Ky.
Proved by oath of William McKenzie.
Legatees: brother Otway, to have $10. ; sister Jane
Price, to have $10; to brother Peter Bailey, $10;
sister Elizabeth A. Harrelson, gold watch and chain;
sister-in-law, Evelina Bailey, a riding horse; to brother Francis Bailey and sister Elizabeth Harrelson,
all estate in Mississippi and Kentucky.

LEGGETT, ABSALOM.

Probated 22 July, 1835.
Sons: Right, to have money; Absalom, to have land;
James; heirs of John L. Leggett, dec'd.
Daughter: Anny. Legatees: Peter Weems, Thomas Walker,
John Smith, to have $5. a piece.
Exr: Col. Peter Perkins (friend).
Wit: H.J.C. Ready, Nicholas Tomler, John Allen, Jared
Way.

DOBBS, JOHN.

No dates--------
Wife: Leah, to have $1,000. Children: Sarah, Elizabeth,
James, Henry and Jackson.
Daughters: Eliza Mims and Mary Ross, to receive $1,000.
each. Sons to receive a $1,000. each, as they come of age.
Daughters: Sarah, Elizabeth and Isabella Dobbs, to have
$1,000. each. Exrs: wife, Jesse Mims, G. Ross, Daniel
McCalep. Wit: Daniel McCalep, Alexander McCalep, Henry
Walthall.

Powell

POWER, ANSEL.

Feb. 19, 1834. September Court, 1835.
Children: Luther, Edwin (or Edward), Calvin, Henry, Will-
is, Alfred, Ale and Clarissa. (wife)
Alfred Moon named as guardian of children.
Wit: G.E. Beauchamp, R.J. Townes.

SMITH, DAVID.

August 21, 1826. December, 1835.
Children: Sarah Humphrey (dec'd), late wife of George
Humphrey; Polly Gibson, wife of David Gibson; Sarah Ter-
ry, wife of Joseph K. Terry; F.W.N.A. Smith, Benjamin F.
Smith; Josiah C. Smith; Esther Crutcher (dec'd), wife of
George Crutcher; Obedience A. Runnells, wife of Hiram G.
Runnells; establishes a fund for youngest dau., Emeline
Smith. Exrs: Obedience Smith (wife), sons Benjamin and
Josiah Smith.
Wit: Benjamin Hatcher, F.G. Hopkins, Thomas Newell.

BELL, ROBERT H.

No dates.
Wife: Susan M. Bell. Daughter: Susan Cordelia Bell.
Estate to wife and daughter, but should wife and daughter
die, brother, Isaac Bell, to have 1/3 of estate and 2/3
to be divided between brothers John and Thomas Bell,
sisters, Nancy Wilson, Polly White and heirs of Nancy

Crawford (dec'd.); 2 daughters of James Bell (dec'd),
Charlotte Corday and Mary Bell. Slave, Vincent, to have
his freedom and $100. in cash to bear expenses to a free
state. Exr: brother Isaac Bell, also named as guardian of
dau. Susan C. Bell.
Wit: I.R. Nicholson, Sam Brown, Henry G. Johnston.

TERRELL, JONATHAN.

July 27, 1835. Sept. Court, 1835.
Wife: mentioned, but not named. Sons: Andrew, to have
160 acres of land; Jonathan to have one small negro and
$100. Wit: Wash Pleasant.

LEE, SHERROD.

April 14, 1835. September, 1835.
Wife: Rachel. Children: William James, Alexander, Eliza-
beth, Samuel Coleman and unborn child.
Exr: William Cranes. Wit: William Lowe, Meday Bozeman.

RATLIFF, SIMPSON.

October 5, 1834. November Court, 1834.
Wife: Catherine, to raise and educate children, towit:
William E., Anna and James W. When son William arrives
at the age of 21 years, to have his part of estate.
Exrs: wife, Levy H. Tatum, William Ratliff.
Wit: William Thomas Stovall, John Ratliff, William Spencer.

GOODSON, WILLIAM.

Feb. 28, 1834. November, 1834.
Wife: Elizabeth, to have slaves, cattle, horses, $500.
To daughter, Martha Dorner Goodson, all my estate, real
and personal, that 1 now have, and negroes, should she
die without issue the property to go to granddaughter,
Susan Ellen Collins and Rachel Sherwood.
Exrs: John A. Fairchild, Joseph Ross, James Scott.
Wit: Carg C. Page, Powers Scott, J.L.P.Stranger.

SMITH, SAMUEL.

October 12, 1833. Jan. 26, 1835.
Dau: Margaret Jane Hume, to have $50.
Balances of property to wife, Mary O. Smith, to support
our children- William Dinsmore Smith, Catherine Eliza
Smith and Susan Ellen Smith, Martha Ditts Smith.
Exr: Joseph A. McKanen (?).
Wit: Robert Leeper, K.M.Osborne, T.L.Osborne.

HAUGE, SAMUEL.

August 26, 1837. Jan. 28, 1838.
Legatees: daughter, Elizabeth Hickenbotham, to have 3
slaves; dau. Susannah Curtis, slaves ; son William, slaves;
son Samuel, slaves; Hannah (slave), to have her freedom.
Exr: son William. Wit: Edmund Frenches, D. Mathewson.

WHITAKER, ABRAHAM.

Nov. 13, 1837. December Court, 1838.
Estate to be divided between wife, Frances, and children.
Exrs: Orvell Whitaker and Ebenezer Divine.
Wit: William Cabean, Robert Wells, George Harrell.

STEWART, JOHN.

1858---
Victoria County, Texas.
Sons: William B., to have $50. in cash; John H., to have
slaves; Andrew, to have slaves; Charles A., to have slaves
and $500. in money. Exrs: sons Andrew Stewart and Charles
Stewart. Wit: William Glass, W.L.Harrison.

BIRDSON, WILLIAM.

Sept. 9, 1836. June 2, 1837.
Legatees: dau. Ann Elizabeth, to have all of estate;
sister Ann M. Wall, to have saddle horse; bro. George
Birdson, to have a watch; neice Mary Ann Holeman (dau. of
William Holeman, now of Wight Co., Va.)to have $5000. in
the event of death of daughter.

TALBOT, JAMES.

Sept.1837. Sept. Court, 1837.
Nuncupative will. All estate to 2 youngest sisters.

MONROE, JENNETT.

July 24, 1837. October, 1837.
Legatees: Angus McInnis to pay to heirs of daughter, Kath-
erine McInnis; Malcolm Monroe, to divide money among heirs
of beloved dau. Margaret Monroe; to heirs of dau. Jennett---
; Arabella Stewart, to have a negro; Samuel and John Watson
to have a negro; Mary McLean (niece).
Exr: Daniel Stewart (brother).
Wit: John Morrison, Roderick McDuffin.

BOYKINS, JOHN.

Nov. 10, 1836. October, 1837.
Wife: Catherine, to have slaves.
Sons: Simon, William, John, Drury Debury.
Daughter:Nancy Harrison.
Wit: Alfred Eldridge, Isaiah W. Parker.
Exrs: son John P., William H. Harrison (of Southhampton
County, Virginia.

HARDIN, DAVID.

Jan. 8, 1824. 1824.
Of Orange Co., N.C.
Sons: John, William and Thomas, all to have slaves.
Daughters: Dolly Wells, Elizabeth C-----, Sally, Martha.
Gr.dau: Winifred Thompson.
Exrs: Winny Hardin (wife), Sally Hardin, W. Shaw.
Wit: Mills Wells, A. Moore, John Moore.

MOORE, ALFRED.

Probated March, 1837.
Children: George (eldest son), to be sent to the Univer-
sity of North Carolina; land to be divided between sons
George and David; dau. Delia, to be educated and have a
slave. Legatees: Luther, Edward, Calvin and Alfred Powell,
each to have a negro. Land purchased from brother William
Moore to be sold.
Exrs: John Mikle (brother-in-law), William N. Robinson.

KELLAM, BOWDOIN.

April 29, 1837. May, 1837.
Daughters: Mary Ann Evans (wife of A.D.Evans), Elizabeth
Jones (wife of John Jones). 2/3 of estate to Mary Ann
Evans and 1/3 to Eliza Jones, they to have income from
estate during their life time.
Exrs: Jacob Fort and Peter Sanders.

JOPLING, JESSE.

Dec.2, 1834. March Court, 1837. Of Amherst Co., Va.
Holeman Jopling (cousin) to have 300 acres of land.
George Thomas, to have $1000. over and above anything
I may owe him, $2000. to be paid him after settlement
of estate. Chester Ingle, sometimes called Chester Jop-
ling, a tract of land in Nelson County (Virginia) and
residue of estate . Chester and Allen Ingle to pay $50.
per month to their mother during her life.
Exrs: Chester Jopling, Reuben Patterson.
(Will was probated in Albemarle County, Virginia).

EDWARDS, MONTALBUT.

Oct. 19, 1836. December Court, 1836.
Wife: Elizabeth, to have slaves, land and personal
property. Exrs: wife, Richard Edwards (brother).
Wit: James Hall, R.H. Turnbull, J.R. Nicholson.

CATHELL, JONATHAN.

Probated January Court, 1837.
Estate bequeathed to brother, James Cathell.
Wit: Daniel Williams, J.B. Fairchild.

BOZEMAN, MEDAY.

Probated   ---1837.
Wife: Jane.   Children: Nancy Jane, Elizabeth and Joel,
to live with uncle Thomas Bozeman, who is named as guardian.   Exrs: James Bozman (brother), Simeon Barton.
Wit: Charles Woodworth, William Roberts, Nancy Barfiels.

KILBORN, JAMES B.

Feb. 1837.   Feb. 1837.
Wife: Susan Wilson Kilborn, to have use of all of estate.
Son: James G. Kilborn.
Exr: wife.
Wit: W.T.Turnell, H.H. Armstrong, E.V.H. Perkins.
Codicil to will gives to daughter of Nancy Walton (wife of
Robert L. Walton), slaves.

JOPLING, THOMAS.

August, 1789. Sept. Court, 1789. Of Amherst Co., Virginia.
Wife: Hannah, to have land and slaves.
Gr.son: Jesse, to have land after decease of wife Hannah.
Sons: James, Josiah and Thomas Jopling.
Exrs: sons James and Josiah.
Wit: Henry Morton, Joseph Thomas, Thomas Farrar, John Cop-
ling. (Copy of above will filed in Hinds County, 1837)

BAIRD, FELIX W.

December 5, 1835. May 1836.
Wife: Harriett, to have slaves.
Dau: Isabella Baird, slaves and 1000 acres of land.
"I will that my boy, Tom, (slave) be emancipated, provi-
ded with necessary clothing etc."Mention is made of land
in North Carolina. To friend, M.A.Gillespie, my pony.

Friend, S.C.Barton, to have watch and pistol.
Mark A. Gillespie, guardian of dau. Isabella, she to be
sent to Salem, North Carolina, to school. Should daughter
die, property to go to M.A. Gillespie and Simeon C. Barton.
Wit: Humphrey Stewart, Lemuel Edmonson, N.W. Vallingham.

ROBINSON, RAYMOND.

Feb. 13, 1836. May, 1836.
Estate left to 2 daughters.
Exrs: Elizabeth Caldwell, Lucy Downs (daughters), James R.
Robinson (nephew).
Wit: E.W. Harring, James B. Robinson, Henry G. Johnston.

CALDWELL, ISAAC.

Feb. 27, 1829.   Feb., 1836.
Estate to wife Elizabeth and son Raymond.
Exrs: wife, James B. Robinson (friend).

PERVIS, JAMES P.J.

Feb. 9, 1836. Feb. Court, 1836.
Wife: Elizabeth, to have 1/2 of estate, and James B.M.
Pervis and Mary Ann Pervis (children) to have other half.
Exrs: wife and Besolia Campbell (father-in-law).
Wit: F.E.Plummer.

COFFEE, HIRAM.

1836------
Wife: Elizabeth, to have the sum of $20,000.
Legatees: Green Coffee (half-bro.), to have $15,000.;
nieces and nephews (children of bro.-in-law William
Edmonson, dec'd.), to have $1,000. each.
Exrs: Thomas F. Coffee and Joseph A. McRaven (?).
Wit: Orin C. Dow, Thomas J. Coffee, Colley McDaniel,
D.N. Haley.

PENDLETON, RICE.

Jan. 24, 1836. Feb. Court, 1836.
Children: Jane, Mary and Malvina Pendleton.
Exrs: Willis Landrum, of Virginia (bro.-in-law), William
M. Rives, of Miss.   Wit: James Wydown, William Morson.

LAWHON, WILLIAM.

Feb. 11, 1836. Feb. Court, 1836.

Son: Daniel Henry Lawhon.
Executrix: Elizabeth Lawhon (wife).
Wit: David Hendrick, Jared May, Stancel L. Walker.

PULLIAM, THOMAS.

Legatees: sister Jerusha Cawthorne, for love and affection
I bear her, to have #1. ; sister Frances Cawthorne, to
have $100. ; sisters Nancy Earkins, Sarah Avery, Keseck
McKay, Jemina Pulliam, each to have $1.00 ; brother Benja-
min Pulliam, to have a tract of land.
Wit: Samuel B. Daughty and Thomas Spell.

GRAVES, JOHN.

Sept. 17, 1836. Sept. Court, 1836.
Legatees: brother Thomas Graves, to have tavern and land
in the town of Brandon and a lot of Irish whiskey that is
on the way from Ireland ; brother James Graves and sister
Catherine.   Wit: Robert Hughes, William H. Young, John
Long.

WILLIAMS, WILLIAM.

October 1, 1836. October Court, 1836.
Legatees: brother Andrew P. Williams, to have half of the
estate and sister Elizabeth Powell, the other half. Bro.
Andrew said to be a citizen of Missouri.
Exr: Joseph Stephenson. Wit: A.A. Clark, J.E.Cowan.

WELLS, GEORGE.

June 10, 1836. October, 1836.
Legatees: son John, to have land and slaves; son Napoleon
to have land and slaves; son Thomas, land and slaves; dau.
Eliza Stanard, slaves; dau. Catherine Wells, slaves; dau.
Elinor Wells, slaves; daus. Cynthia Ann, Eliza, Catherine
and Elinor, to have $500 each. Exrs: sons John and Thomas.
Wit: Isaac Selser, Elizabeth Selser and Letitia Selser.

FLUKER, DAVID.

March 30, 1835. Dec. 26, 1835.
Wife: Isabella, to have land, slaves and personal property.
Son: David, to have $5.
Wit: William Stewart, Jr., H. Epperson, James Jones.

SCOTT, JACOB.

August 29, 1835.   December 26, 1835.
Negro woman and her child Sarah are to be set free. In
order that this part of my will may be carried into
effect, it is my wish that my executors apply to legislature of state for an act confirming the emancipation
of said negroes by virtue of will. $1,000 to be spent
by executors in manner the said Legislature may divert
and appoint for use and benefit of said negroes.
The rest and residue of estate bequeathed to mother,
Phebe Scott, of Chesterfield County, Virginia.
Exrs: Dr. William H. Young and Col. John Grumbell (or
Grumball). Wit: R.J. Townes and S.F. Noble.

Allen, James B.   --   -- Elizabeth Jackson
Alfred, John   --   -- Rebecca Lowe
Anderson, I.   --   -- Hanna Wood
Allbruton, William --   -- Anna Catchings
Anderson, M.   --   -- Elizabeth Kelly
Alford, Jesse   --   -- Polly Ratberry (?)

"B"

Bryant, Nathan   --   -- Martha A. Cameron
Bowles, Wesley   --   -- Sarah Ann Walton
Brown, Jeremiah   --   -- Margaret McAlpin
Benton, Joseph   --   -- Elizabeth Mobley
Betsel, John   --   -- Jane Anderson
Bogen, James   --   -- Laura Mitchell
Brown, George   --   -- Martha Perry
Brackenridge, M.L. --   -- Elizabeth Dawson
Barwell, Nathaniel --   -- Martha Ross
Buckner, E.   --   -- Jane E. Far
Barksdale, Malcolm --   -- Sarah Everett
Barrett, Oliver   --   -- Sarah Walton
Brewer, William   --   -- America Taylor
Battle, Elisha   --   -- ----------
Blake, E.H.   --   -- M.M. Harris
Bradley, A.P.   --   -- -------
Blanchard, N.T.   --   -- E.A. Robinson
Browning, B.A.   --   -- Charlotte Parker
Blackburn, D.   --   -- E. Harris
Bush, Hiram   --   -- P.E. Clark
Brown, William   --   -- Jane Duncam
Brown, Drury   --   -- Sarah Wells
Bird, Samuel   --   -- Sarah Ford

"C"

Carvil, Joseph B.   --   -- Caroline Evans
Crisler, B.   --   -- Juliana Porter
Cotting, Nelson   --   -- Patsy Gordon
Carter, Nelson   --   -- Mary Sims
Carter, David   --   -- Sarah Munger
Castleman, S.   --   -- Elvira Harvey
Cook, Lazarus   --   -- Adaline Roberts
Callahan, John   --   -- Elizabeth Dickerson
Cottingham, Jonathan --   -- M-----
Catchings, Jonathan --   -- M. Gallsmans
Catlett, F.   --   -- R. Hadley
Clovers, Daniel   --   -- Patsy Hood.

Colton	--	Johnson
Chapman, S.	-- --	M. Britton
Cooper, William	----	Clara Wardell
Clark, Gipson	----	Eliza A. Truly

"D"

Dills, George	----	Martha McRaven
Davis, George	----	Nancy Moore
Downing, Thomas, Jr.	----	Elizabeth Crane
Davis, Josiah	----	Sarah Kent
Dennis, Josiah	----	Phebe Granberry
Dunn, A.W.	----	Amelia Breeden
Dodd, John B.	----	H.M.Ward
Davis, John	----	Mary F. Brown
Dilworth, George	----	L. Throckmorton

"E"

E' anks, Lem	----	Mary Allem
Evans, Jesse	----	Jane Carvill
Ellis, William	----	Mary T. Battle
Evans, L.S.	----	Miss Bell
Ewing, Willis	----	Mary J. Ross
Ellison, Henry	----	Sarah Ann Battle

"F"

Flowers, James	-----	Jane King
Ford, Ferdinand	----	Elizabeth C. Whitford
Freeman, Elijah	-----	Esther Jackson
Felps, James	----	Margaret Felps
Faulkner, S.C.	----	Mary Flournoy
Femor, Loryn	----	Nancy Alford
Farris, Willis A.	----	B. Whitesides
Foster -----	----	Susan -----
Finchep, Samuel	----	E. Pope
Fluker, David	----	Isabella Davis
Fortner, Benjamin	----	Ellen Mullins

"G"

Gibbs, Wilmot	----	Sarah Montgomery
Glass, David	----	Sarah Fall
Granberry, L.	----	Rebecca Harrell
Goddard, Thomas	----	Ann Buckholdt
Granberry, H.	----	Elizabeth Joyce
Green, Thomas	----	Harriett Lamar
Gallman, Jesse	----	Rebecca Philips
George, William	----	Miss Battle
Goff, I.D.	----	P. McKay
Golberry, John	----	Salina Stacy

"H"

Haxhall, Newton L.	----	Sarah Ragland
Hamer, William	----	A.I.Robinson
Harrington, Young	----	Nancy Magee
Harly, M.	----	Eliza Goode
Hume, John	----	Margaret Smith
Harrison, Michael	----	Martha Veach
Horton, A.V.	----	Sarah Farquar
Howze, W.	----	Catherine Bennett
Hall, R.	----	Lucinda Phillips
Haslep, David	----	Elizabeth Edwards
Hooten, James	----	Nancy Smith
Holmes, C.	----	Mary Waterhouse
Henderson, J.M.	----	M. Andrews
Hardwick, Josiah	----	Lydia Taber
Haffington, I.G.	----	Mary J. Pettimore
Huff, L.	----	R. Morgan
Holiday, S.E.	----	Marian Griffith
Hollingsworth---	----	------Miller
Hinkley, George	-----	Elizabeth Lang
Hargroves, J.A.	----	A. Parker
Hopkins, John	----	Elizabeth A. Napier
Head, Thomas	----	J.B. Sharkey
Hall, William	----	Sally Shepherd
Hawkins, John B.	----	Clarissa Henley
Hudson, Henry.	----	Elizabeth Allen
Holt, Robert	----	Harriet Sturgis
Hutchinson, A.	----	M.X. Collin
Hardin, S.H.	----	Jane Wilson
Hunter, Henry	----	-----------
Hawley, John	----	S.E.Dresser

"I"

Ince, Francis (?)	----	M.B.Granberry
Ivey, Thomas	----	Lydia Keen

"J"

Jones, John	----	Eliza Burnot
Johnston ---	----	Amanda King
Jones, William	----	Mary Senna
Judd, Selah	----	Elisa Heaily
Jackson, James	----	A. Simpson
Johnson, M.	----	S. Williams
Jackson----	-----	Miss Cox
Johnson, William	----	Lena Goode
Jopling, Allen	----	Martha Simpson

"K"

King, Charles	----	Louisa Carter
Katch, John	----	Elizabeth Santo
Kirkpatrick, E.	----	M.H. Jones (?)
Kinkaid, C.A.	-----	Miss Roberts
Keenan, Francis	----	Miss Richey

"R"

Redwine, Percy	----	Dina Garner
Robinson, R.	----	Sarah Waldrop
Rose, George	----	Sarah Stone
Roberts, William	----	Margaret Bozeman
Radcliff, William	----	Jane Davis
Ross, William	----	Elizabeth Bird
Robertson, J.W.	----	S.C.Carson

"S"

Strother, Walter	----	Prudence Yesser
Slaid, James	----	Susan Cooper
Sims, G. Benjamin	----	W.I.Moffett
Stewart, James	----	Emily Bolton
Stewart, John	----	Jane Watson
Stanard, William	----	E.C.Adams
Stratton, Jesse	----	--------

"T"

Thatcher, George W.	--	Sarah Montgomery
Theypen, James	--	Mahaly Easterly
Tharp, George	---	Martha Ballard
Thomas, William	---	Susanna Jones
Thompson, Samuel	---	C. Granberry
Throckmorton, James	---	E. Weise
Taber, Carrol	----	Laura Williams
Thornton, Mili	----	Sarah Easterling

"U"

Ussery, John	---	Molly Khansoy(?)

"V"

Van Arsdoll	---	Mary Milnor
Vanderpool, Cornelius	---	Elizabeth Hammett

(This list of Hinds County marriages is incomplate.)

JOHNSTON, AARON.

Nov. 25, 1819. **Admr:** Robert Mathis.
Bondsmen: Willis Vick, Foster Cook

BOYD, JAMES.

November 29, 1819. Admr: James Steele.
Bondsmen: Francis Griffin and Benjamin Lansdell.

FORTNER, THOMAS.

February 28, 1820. Admr: Polly Fortner.
Bondsmen: John Mathis, Isaac Raplje, Westley Mathis.

HYLAND, JACOB.

1819---- Admr: John Brian.
BONDSMEN: William Rushing, Russell Smith.

COLEMAN, ROBERT.

April 1, 1820. Admr: William P. Coleman.
Bondsmen: Thomas Gravals, Russell Smith.

SCARLETT, JAMES.

July 31, 1820. Admr: Robert McClure, also named as
guardian for Brice, Leonora and Emily Scarlett.
Bondsmen: Levi Mitchell and Jordan Gibson.

COOK, EDWIN.

October 25, 1819. Admr: Foster Cook.
Bondsmen: Foster Cook, Willis B. Vick, B. Wrenn.
"Whereas Edwin Cook, late of said county, deceased,
having while he lived and at the time of his decease, divers goods, right and credits within the
county and state aforesaid, and leaving no will and
testament behind and we desiring that goods, rights
and credits of said deceased may be well and truly
administered, converted and disposed of, do hereby
grant unto said Foster Cook administration of estate."

SMITH, LUCIUS.

October 25, 1819.
Russell Smith, Andrew Glass, Henry Downs, are named
bondsmen for Russell Smith, who is guardian for minor
children of Lucius Smith- Eleanor, Benjamin F. and
Meranda Smith.

DEES, SAMPSON.

Probated Sept. 23, 1817. Of Christian County, Kentucky.
Wife: Ruth, to have household goods and 2 negroes.
Children: son Samuel (youngest) to have negro, horse,
saddle and bridle, feather bed and household furniture;
dau. Polly Dees, to have negro, horse and saddle; dau.
Altezes Woolf, to have negro, horse and saddle; sons
William, Danson (Denson), Luke; daus. Elizabeth Fisher
and Sally Jones. Exr: wife
Wit: John Clark, John Polls, John Mancy, David Mancy.

LANE, JOSEPH.

August 20, 1824. October 25, 1824.
Legatees: Mrs. Louisa Ford (friend) and Simon Lane
(brother). Exr: John Lane (friend)
Wit: Thomas Anderson, Jeff Nailer.

MCELRATH, THOMAS.

Probated Sept. 27, 1825.·   Admr: Benjamin Bedford.
Bondsmen: William McD. Pettit, Archibald Erwin.

FERGUSON, SARAH.

Probated Sept. 8, 1825.
Legatees: Joseph Ferguson (bro.); Susan Brown (sister);
Matilda Ferguson (sister); Sally Cowan (niece); James
C. Jones (nephew); dau. Emily Ferguson, to have land
and negroes.   Exr: Henry W. Vick.
Wit: John Cameron, Joel Powell, Gray J. Vick.

DANIEL, THOMAS

Jan. 26, 1824.   Admrs: Nancy Daniel, John Sevier and
M. Spann.

CAMERON, DUNCAN.

Oct. 25, 1824· Admrs: Joel Cameron, Jacob Hyland.

RAGSDALE, BENJAMIN.

27 October, 1823.
Admrs: Mary Ragsdale, Joseph Templeton, Levi Mitchell.

COGGINS, PASCHAL.

December 23, 1823.
Admrs: Allen Sharkey, Charles Gee.

John Ritchey and Randolph Palmer, appointed guardian
of Edward Hale Mitchell. Sept. 22, 1823.

LORIMER, JOHN.

October 19, 1821.
"I, John Lorimer, of Charlotte Street, in Parish of
St. Mary Soban, in the county of Middlesex, Doctor of
Physics. I bequeath unto and forgive the payment by
my brother, Patrick Stratham, of Drumdurm, in the county of Elgin." Wife: Katherine, to have money, and
after her decease the money to be put in trust to educate a boy of relations of my father and mother.
Late father was John Lorimer. (A long and unusal will)

MCLEOD, MURDOCK.

Nov. 24, 1823. Admrs: John Henderson, John Lane, Charles
Henderson.

BOOKER, WILLIAM.

Nov. 8, 1822. Nov. 28, 1823. (Of Claiborne Co., Miss.)
Estate to wife, Susan Booker, and infant children- James
and Sally Booker. Exrs: wife, Allen Sharkey.
Wit: Stephen McLean, Levi Primon

HUNTER, PLEASANT.

April 28, 1823. Admrs: Foster Cook, Joseph Templeton.

WHITE, DEMSEY.

April 21, 1823.
Wife: Hannah, to have 2 cows, four dollars in cash,
1 roan horse, saddle, bridle, 1 bed and furniture.
Rest of estate to be divided between sons and daughters. Exrs: son Nathan White and Edward Cook.

BLANCHARD, JOHN.

June 24, 1823·
Admrs: Elizabeth Blanchard, L.L. Blanchard, Green Edwards·

CASH, ROBERT·

Sept. 22, 1823.
Admrs: Robert Boardman, H.F. Schweppe.

GLASS, ANDREW.

Sept.22, 1823.
Admrs: Polly Glass, Jacob Hyland.

Miller, Charles.

October, 1819.
Admr: Foster Cook. Bondsmen: Foster Cook, Richard Hawkins, Bellfield Wrenn.

PERLEY, JOHN.

Oct. 25, 1819. Admr: James Steele. Bondsmen: Seth Griffth and Henry Maynader.

ARCHER, JAMES.

October 25, 1819. Admrs: Seth Griffith.
Bondsmen: Josiah Griffith and Russell Smith.

John Rail is appointed guardian of Willis Sharp and James Sharp. Bondsmen: John Rail, R. Smith, Murphy Bradford.

GREENLEAF, DAVID.

---1819. Admr: John Greenleaf. Bondsmen: Andrew Glass, Francis Griffin.

DEES, SAMPSON.

October 25, 1819. Admr: Ruth Dees. Bondsmen: Francis Griffin, Andrew Glass, Henry Downs. (Bond $800.)

FRYER, AARON.

Admrs: Nancy Fryer, James Fryer, Moses Evans, Claudius Rawls.

Henry Downs appointed guardian for infant children of James Scarlett. December 28, 1818.

COOK, JOHN.

Jan. 4, 1819. Admr: Bellfield Wrenn.
Bondsmen: James Knowland and Patrick Sharkey.

WELLS, WILLIAM D.

April, 1818.   Admr: Robert Ferrall.
Bondsmen: Robert L. Mathis and James Higgins.

HOWING, GEORGE.

Probated Feb. 14, 1826.
Brothers: William Howing (of Samson, N.C.), Benjamin Howing (Miss.), James Howing and Nathan Howing.
Sisters: Mary and Jane (of North Carolina).
Exr: Bion Sepion (or Sesion).
Wit: Mabry Spann, Wilson Phipps, Robert M. Spann.

WILLIAMS, ELIZABETH.

Probated. · Jan. 16, 1826.
Slaves bequeathed to friend, Jordon Gibson, who has befriended me in my old age.
Wit: Randal Gibson, William Shaw, Robert Hatcher, James Gibson.

CLOYD, JOSEPH.

October 3, 1826.
Admrs: Elizabeth Robinson and Henry Downs.

HICKEY, JAMES.

May 28, 1821. Admr: Robert McClure.
Bondsmen: Russell Smith, Thomas B. Tompkins.

DAVIS, JEREMIAH.

Sept. 24, 1821. Admr: Wiley Davis.
Bondsmen: William Rushing, John Coward.

FERGUSON, JAMES.

Sept. 24, 1821. Admr: Feriby Ferguson.
Bondsmen: William Rushing, John Cowan, Wiley Davis.

JORDAN, DANIEL.

October 8, 1821. Admr: Pharaoh Knowland.
Bondsmen: Anthony Durden, James Gibson.

FORD, FREDERICK.

October 9, 1821. Admr: Francis Griffins.
Bondsmen: Andrew Glass, Levi Mitchell.

VICK, NEWIT.

October 9, 1821. Admr: John Lane.
Bondsmen: W. Blanton, Reuben Newman, Jacob Hyland.

Jacob Hyland appointed guardian for Levi Gibson, infant
heir of Stephen Gibson. Bondsmen: Andrew Glass, James
Hyland, Allen Sharkey.

GALLOWAY, ROBERT.

November 26, 1821.   Admrs: Margaret and Thomas Galloway. Bondsmen: Francis Griffin, Andrew Glass.

WALTERS, HORACE G.

December 31, 1821.   Admr: Joseph Templeton.
Bondsmen: Seth N. Griffith, Levi Mitchell.

Elijah Ragsdale, guardian of John and Sally Fortner,
infant heirs of Vincent Fortner. Bondsmen: John
Mathis, Samuel Savoy. Dec. 31, 1821.

BRADFORD, HENRY.

Jan. 8, 1822. Admr: Murphy Bradford.
Bondsmen: Green Edwards and Russell Smith.

WATSON, EVERETT.

October 28, 1822.   Admrs: Jeremiah Watson, Samuel
Mason, Jordon Gibson.

TRAVIS, THOMAS.

November 25, 1822. Admr: Baler Travis.
Bondsmen: Mathew B. Sellers, Andrew Glass, Bellfield
Wrenn.

HOLLINGSWORTH, WILLIAM.

December, 1822. Admr: Barnet Hollinsworth.
Bondsman: Reuben Newman.

COOK, EDWIN.

Dec. 22, 1822. Admrs: Winnifred Cook, Robert Boardman.

Morris Murphy appointed guardian of Alexander and Sarah
McLeod.

HAMER, CHARLES.

Sept. 6, 1816. Oct. 31, 1820.
Wife: Elizabeth, to manage the estate until oldest child
reaches age of eighteen years. 5 children, but not named.
Exr: wife. Wit: Thomas E. McElrath, Francis Canfield,
Raymond Robinson.

COOK, ALEXANDER.

Probated May 24, 1820.
Wife: Sarah, to have one part of estate with children.
Exrs: wife, Reuben Newman (friend)
Wit: Hartwell Vick, Margaret Cook, Silvia Vick.

Margaret Cook appointed administratrix and guardian
of Cecilia and M. J. Cook, infant heirs of John Cook,
dec'd. Bondsmen: Robert M. Spann, Russell Smith. Jan.
29, 1821.

STEPHENS, THOMAS.

----1829. Admr: John Stephens.
Bondsmen: Britton Stephens, John Mathis.

HUGHES, JAMES.

Oct. 5, 1819. Jan. 28, 1821.
Children: James, Elijah, Morin and Greenbury.

Exrs: friends, William Whitfield, Robert Haning, Robert
Galloway. Wit: R. Smith, Randolph Palmer, George Palmer.

BROWN, JAMES.

Probated. Nov. 9, 1820.
Wife: Elizabeth.   Children: sons Jeremiah and Jacob
Brown (youngest), to have land and negroes; son Benjamin, to have negro; dau. Elizabeth, personalty and
negroes; dau, Nancy Brown, to have 2 negroes and feather bed; dau. Jane Williamson, to have $250. ; dau. Cath-
erine Aleford, to have $250.; 3 youngest children- Nan-
cy, Jeremiah and Jacob- to be educated.
Exrs: wife and friend James Gibson.
Wit: Zephanie Cood, Thomas Tompkins, Roger Glass.

BLACK, ALEXANDER.

May 27, 1822. Admr: Elizabeth Black.
Bondsmen: William Whitfield, Russell Smith.

Nimrod R. Selser and William Hyland guardians to Sarah
Wright. June 3, 1822.

WHITTINGTON, LEVI.

July 22, 1822. Admr: Amelia Whittington.
Bondsmen: Christopher Hyland and Russell Smith.

BISHOP, ROBERT M.

All estate to father, Lovett Bishop, and brother Isaac
N. Bishop (both of Morgan County, Ohio).
Exr: friend Bellfield Wrenn.
Wit: E.D.Walcott, L.B. Hawley, James N. Pittman.

MCLEOD, MURDOCK.

March 31, 1821.
Mentions that he is guardian of first wife's child-
ren. Mention is made of present wife, but not named.
Son Malcolm is only child named.
Exrs: friends Thomas Muckleworth, Andrew Glass.
Wit: Charles Gee and Elizabeth M. Hamer.

WHITE, WILLIAM.

April 4, 1822. Admr: Reuben White.
Bondsmen: Nathan White and Foster Cook.

LEWIS, WILLIAM.

Sept. 30, 1819.
Legatees: Mary Boler (cousin) to have $1000.
To Octavia Boler (dau. of Mary Boler), $500.
To beloved friend, Absalom Boler, one quarter section
of land purchased of Seth Griffin.
To beloved daughter Katherine Grayson, all remaining
part of property, real and personal. Reserving 1/6
of property to be given Susan Grayson (dau. of Kath-
erine), when she reaches age of fourteen years.
Exrs: William Whitfield, Francis Griffin, James Know-
land. Wit: William Whitfield, Glass Goofny(?) and
Francis Hartley.

VICK. NEWELL.

August 2, 1819. (Forty-four years of American Indepen-
dence·)· Wife: Elizabeth, to have share of all estate,
both real and personal· Estate to be divided when son
Wesley reaches age of 21 years.
Sons: Wesley, William, Newell and Hartwell.
Exrs: wife, son Hartwell, Willis B. Vick (nephew).
Wit: Foster Cook, Edwin Cook, B.Vick.
Oct. 25, 1819. Will of Newell Vick probated in court
by surviving executor, proved by the oath of Foster
Cook and Willis Vick. Bond acknowledged in sum of $70,000.

MITCHELL, EDWARD.

June 27, 1831.
Legatees: 3 slaves to be given $50· each, liberated
and sent to the state of Ohio; $1000· to be given 3
boys I have liberated; Elizabeth Sims, to have $5,000:
Ferdinand Sims, to have $1,000.; Eldridge Greenwood, to
have $2,000.; Thomas Greenwood, to have $1,000.; James
Greenwood to have $1,000; Andrew Sims, to have $1,000;
George Brumgard, to have watch; A.G. McNutt, to have
pistols. After legacies are paid and my remains hand-
somely interred, the rest of my estate to be divided between the followin: David Mitchell, William Sims, Elizabeth Sims, Sarah Sims and James Greenwood.
Exrs: Felix Bosworth and Felix Sims.
Wit: A. Haynes, C.R. Nutt, I.P. McNutt.

ELLIOTT, ROBERT.

June 11, 1833.   ----------
Legatees: wife Minerva and brother William.
Exrs: wife, bro. William, Herbert W. Hill (bro·-in-law).
Wit: William B. Pryor, Richard Bolling, Harriet Hill.

136

WRENN, JONES.

March 26, 1832.
Wife, to have household, kitchen furniture, slaves and
land.   Dau: Susan Spann, to have a large number of slaves.
Dau: Margaret Cook, a large number of slaves.
Dau: Jane M. Spann (Henry Spann and Benjamin Newman to act
as trustees for dau. Jane).
Dau: Eliza Spann, slaves and land.
Son: Henry to have land and slaves (Frederick Spann and
Thomas Randolph to act as trustee for son Henry).
Dau: Cecilia Wrenn, to have slaves.
Gr.dau: Cecilia Cook, to have support.
Gr.son: James Wrenn Spann, to have slaves.
Exrs: Charles Spann (son-in-law) and Margaret Cook (dau.).

HAWKINS, RICHARD.

March 5, 1834.
Wife: Betsy.   Children: John, Richard, George, Samuel,
Henry, Edward and Sarah Dart.
Exr: Andrew Bolls.   Wit: A.C.Downs, Wilson Bolls and
John McDaniel.

GRESSELL, GEORGE.

April 22, 1829. Of Green County, Alabama.
Wife: Sarah, to have slaves.
Dau: Sarah Thomas, to have carriage, gig, horses, cattle,
hogs, stock, household furniture.
Exrs: wife and John Thomas (son-in-law).
Wit: W.N. Moffett, Edwin Peck, W. Bell.
(This will was probated in Alabama.)

PATTERSON, JOHN.

July 23, 1834. Nuncupative will.
Proved by the oaths of Elisha Parks and John Gardner.
Taken down by James Cornell. Thomas Redwood, Garner
Parks and Job M. Baker to manage the property for only
son, John Patterson.

COODY, ZEPHANIAH.

July 11, 1830.
Sons: Benea, Archibald and John.
Daughters: Caroline, Irena and Pennah Pace.
Exr: father William Henderson.

HUBBELL, ROBERT.

November 4, 1832.
Estate to Martha Hubbell and children, stepdau. Lavina
Hubell. Sisters: Mary, Elira, Charlotte and Martah
Hubell. Exr: wife and friend William R. Campbell.
Will was proved by the oaths of Jonathan Pilmon, James
Cornell and William R. Campbell.

PARR, HENRY. March 12, 1855.
Only daughter and heir, Louisa Ann Parr.
Exr: Martin Heackle·
Wit: Joseph Hegeman, Felix Thompson, J.L. Gervais.

SWANSON, EDWARD.

March 30, 1833.
Wife: Margaret Swanson, to have entire estate.
Exrs: Josiah C. Smith, Robert Garland.

SUTHERLAND, DAVID.

May 8, 1833.
Estate to friend and executor, Peter Scramshaw.
Wit: William Mills.

HARRIS, HARTWELL.

July 7, 1834.
Legatees: Henrietta Harris (dau): Mary Harris (wife?) and
unborn child; Hartwell Harris (nephew), Samuel Morgan, of
Virginia, to have $1000. in place negroes I intended to
give his late wife, Elizabeth; all negroes who desire may
be emancipated and presented to the colonization with
$1000. to defray their expenses.
Exrs: brothers Samuel and Robert Harris.

FRYER, JOHN.

October 16, 1834.
Legatees: David McCalob and James Hunt.
Wit: John Boyd, A. McIntyre.

PHILIPS, SOLOMON.

September 30, 1830.
"In grateful remembrance of the kind friendship displayed
me by Charles Ambler, of North Salem, Westchester County,
New York, at my first setting out on my professional

career, I give and bequeath to him, the aforesaid Charles
Ambler, $200. Sister Elizabeth, wife of Ephiram Jennings,
to have a plantation; sister Fanny, wife of Isaac Wallace,
to have land ; brother Gilbert S. Philips, land ; sister
Minerva, wife of Thomas Caldwell, land; sister Eliza Ann
Philips, land and books; nephew Solomon Jennings (namesake)
son of Ephiram and Elizabeth Jennings, land; nephew James,
son of Isaac and Fanny Wallace, land; nephew Edward Alonzo,
son of brother Gilbert Philips, land; children of Ephiram
and Elizabeth Jennings to have land; brother George Philips
to have medical instruments and books; clothes to be divided between brothers; cousin Esther Crosby, to have a breast
pin. " I should be extremely sorry to offer any temptation
to any of my brothers, sisters or friends living in the
healthy and delightful State of New York, to leave their
native spot and remove to this inhospitable clime, it is
therefore my most ardent desire that none of my legatees,
or their heirs ever remove or settle on the land or any-
where within the baneful influence of the vast Mississippi
swamps. If any of them should come here to attend the settlement of my estate it is best that they come in the fall
and return in the spring, near May."
Body to be interred in the garden between two damson trees,
with brick, covered over with a marble slab, and with tomb-
stone erected with the following inscription: " Here lies
the body of Solomon Close Philips, M.D., a native of New
York, who departed this life ---- day of ---- A.D. 18-- -
in the ----year of his age. Stranger, beware, I left my
native home, I found no better, but found a tomb."
All slaves to be sold to good masters. Col. Sinclair Gervais to act until my brothers arrive.
Wit: Micajah Terrell and Sinclair Gervais.

SHANNON, JOHN.

December .27, 1852.
Nuncupative will. Proved by the oaths of William Bosley,
Jerry Denny and Joseph Sindigrin. Requests that Thomas
Letts and son William Shannon settle business, after
settlement of estate son William to have all the proceeds·
Children in Pennsylvania to have all property in that state.

STEWART, JAMES.

August 14, 1840.
Legatees: sister Adaline Gibson, to have a negro woman;
nephew Winfield Gibson, to have blind horse; to Ann Gibson,
dau. of Randall and Elizabeth Gibson, negro girl.
Exr: Daniel Nailer. Wit: D.G. Rogers, D.B.Nailer.

DANIEL, NANCY.

August 21, 1831.
Son: Robert B. Daniel, mentions other children, but does
not name. Exr: Shem L. Daniel (son).
Wit: A.G.Long, A. Carson and Joel Powell.

ROGERS, STEPHEN.

September 20, 1827.
All of estate to wife, but does not name.
Exrs: Hugh Powell (son-in-law) and Sarah Powell (dau.)
Proved by the oath of Thomas Green.

VICKS, WILLIS.

April 23, 1830.
All estate to Henry W. Vicks and Gray Vicks (brothers).
Wit: George W. Adams and Ralph Regan.
Proved in court by Gray Vicks, executor.

SIMS, JOHN.

No dates.
Legatees: Polly Sims (wife), Polly Sims (dau.), other
children, but not named. Exrs: Samuel Lunn, William Lunn.
Wit: A. Haynes and Shelly B. Treadwell.

BERNEY, RICHARD.

Probated February, 1831. Nun-cupative will.
Estate to Ann Amelia McDaniel and Martha McDaniel, daus.
of John McDaniel. (Richard Berney died at the home of
John McDaniel)· Proved by the oaths of Samuel Beck and
David Higgins.

MCDANIEL, AMBROSE.

March 14, 1831.   April 25, 1831.
Wife: Nancy, to have all estate in negroes and land.
Exrs: wife and John McDaniel (son)·
Wit: Samuel Beck and James D. Walker

HYLAND, EVE.

June 27, 1828. Sept. 15, 1828.
Legatees: children of Henry and Sarah Maynadier, slaves
and silver; dau. Elizabeth Jones, slaves; gr.dau. Elizabeth Jones, slaves; gr.dau. Matilda Jones, slaves; gr.son
John Jones, slaves; gr.dau. Martha Hyland, slaves, bed
and bedclothes; gr.dau. Eliza Glass, slave; gr.dau.Jane

Reaves, slave, feather bed and bed clothes.
Exr: Jacob Hyland (son).
Wit: Levi R. Gibson and Peter Miller.

NEWMAN, SALLY.

September 4, 1830.
Legatees: estate to 4 youngest children- William, Leonard, Osmund and Martha. Should son-in-law William C.Cross
be unfortunate, then his wife, my daughter Adaline, should
have $100. per annum out of yearly income.
Exr: Sarah Newman (friend), also to act as guardian of 4
minor children. Wit: James Blane and Sally R. Newman.

MCCARVELL, JAMES.

November, 1830. Nun-cupative will.
Wife: not named, to have slaves and land.
Son: Washington, to have 2 slaves.
Dau: Emily, to have 3 slaves.
Exrs: Jesse Chaney and Sarah McCarvell (probably wife).
Proved by the oaths of Jesse B. Rogan and John Slater.

MCCLARY, ABRAHAM.

October 31, 1815. April 9, 1827. Of Sevoir County, Tenn.
Wife: Mary
Sons: Payne, Abraham and Seth McClary.
Daughters: Patsy and Sally McClary.
Exr: John Brabston (friend).
(Large estate in Tenn.)

MARRIAGES

Anthony, John -- Sarah Thompson, Nov. 6, 1814
Alright (Albright), Thomas   -- Nancy Evans, April 3, 1817

"B"

Blanton, W.W. -- Harriet McAllister, March 26, 1818
Bolling, William -- Emily Easton, Nov. 6, 1814
Brown, Lampkin -- Zelpha Swarngham, May 17, 1811
Bardslee, James -- Hester Bradley, June 4, 1811
Black, Joseph -- Deliah Chandler, Feb. 26, 1813
Bradshaw, Peter -- Nancy Fowler, June 30, 1813
Blackman, Peter -- Sarah Ford, --1814
Burnham, Gabriel -- Eunice Hicks, June 14, 1815
Barkley, Samuel -- Elizabeth Glass, June 15, 1817

"C"

Collins, Henry -- Polly Flannigan, June 30, 1813
Caston, Green -- Jane Blanchard, Aug. 4, 1814
Cowan, John -- Sarah Jones, Dec. 19, 1817

"D"

Downs, Joshua -- Sarah Clark, April 3, 1812
Dyer, James -- Bartina Nale, June 27, 1812
Dennis, Thomas -- Elizabeth Smith, ------.
Davis, Martin -- Mary Johnston, July 8, 1818

"E"

Edwards, Green -- Elizabeth Blanchard, June 11, 1816

"F"

Fagan, William -- Elizabeth Ryan, Nov. 16, 1814
Ferguson, Joseph -- Catherine Ferguson, Dec. 5, 1810
Ferguson, William -- Elizabeth Treadwell, Dec. 13, 1814
Frye (or Fryer), William -- Polly Duncan, Sept. 1, 1818
Frazier, Moses -- Nancy Lockie, Dec. 16, 1818.

"G"

Galloway, James -- Polly Hatchell, Dec. 10, 1814
Gibson, James -- Frances Gibson, Feb. 14, 1814
Gibson, John -- Milly Downs, July 31, 1815
Grayson, Samuel -- Catherine Green, Jan. 27, 1812
Griffith, Seth -- Lavina Steele, Aug. 12, 1817
Griffith, Francis -- Patsy Downs, Aug. 20, 1817
Guy, Robert -- Mary Clark, May 15, 1813

"H"

Hughes, James   -- Abby Evans, March 24, 1810
Huffman, John   -- Betsy Ferguson, Jan. 16, 1811
Hyland, James   -- Betsy McCord, April 29, 1811
Henning, Robert   -- Tabitha Hallman, April 15, 1812
Harper, Jesse   -- Jane Kirkwood, June 15, 1811
Herring, Simon B.   -- Susan Young, Oct. 17, 1812
Hicks, Benjamin   -- Uncie Brown, Jan. 15, 1814
Hartley, Francis   -- Elizabeth Whitfield ---
Hyland, William   -- Nancy Wright, June 22, 1816
Hammond, Joshua   -- Milly Page, Dec. 18, 1816
Hyland, James   -- Sarah Phillips, Jan. 2, 1817
Houston, John   -- Lavina Lumsford, Sept. 9, 1817

"K"

King, James   -- Elizabeth Crockett, March 27, 1816

"M"

Marsh, Joshua   -- Rhoda Anderson, June 22, 1813
Manadier, Henry   -- Sally Hyland, March 27, 1816
McLeod, Murdock   -- Martha Hamor, Dec. 29, 1816

"O"

Oliver, James   -- Polly Wright, April 16, 1812

"P"

Pearcy, William   -- Harriet Galloway, May 15, 1814

"R"

Rushing, William   -- Elizabeth Griffin, March 3, 1817
Ross, David   -- Elizabeth Walker, June 28, 1817
Robinson, George   -- Lucinda Galloway, Jan. 31, 1818

"S"

Savoy, Lewis   -- Elizabeth Lashley, May 4, 1810
Smith, Thomas   -- Nancy Goodwin, June 29, 1818
Sanders, Green   -- Elizabeth Mason, June 4, 1818
Steele, Isaac   -- Nancy Johnston, June 6, 1818
Sims, Peyton   -- Mary Head, July 21, 1818
Stotts, Abraham   -- Mary Labdell, August 3, 1810
Sheridan, Thomas   -- Margaret Hallam, Sept. 7, 1810
Seay, Howell   -- Margaret Davis, May 11, 1812
Stephens, John   -- Elizabeth Mathis, July 13, 1814
Sharkey, Allen   -- Elizabeth Booker, Jan. 26, 1816
Seveir, John   -- Mary Daniel, April 20, 1816
Smith, Plmy(?)   -- Margaret Houston, March 8, 1816
Sharkey, Patrick   -- Martha Gibson, Nov. 6, 1816

"T"

Thomas, William -- Elizabeth Wright, March 28, 1810
Tuttle, Samuel -- Lena Bradley,   -- 1811
Truman, Arnold -- Lydia Goodwin, May 27, 1816

"U"

Ussery, William -- Mary Burnett, August 6, 1810
Ussery, John -- P --- Hampton, August 14, 1814

"V"

Vickory, Aaron -- name missing- not filled, August 14,
1817. Oliver Dyer, named as bondsman.

"W"

Wilson, John -- Celia Nabb, April 7, 1811
Willis, William -- Martha Vick, May 22, 1816
Wallis, Thomas -- Peggy Locke, March 8, 1817

Anderson, William
Arnett, James

Belfor, John
Bell, Thomas B.
Bemy, John
Bridgers, John
Byers, William W.
Barton, William
Brown, Jesse
Bean, Lemuel
Barrington, George
Belsha, Robert
Barnes, Lilburne
Barnes, William
Brown, Elijah
Byers, John, H.
Barfield, William I.
Barfield, James H.
Barfield, Joel
Brown, J.T.
Boon, John
Bounds, P.H.
Bounds, James
Baity, Abel
Burns, Thomas
Butcher, Joseph
Barnes, John
Buford, R.A.
Baker, Thomas
Benton, William
Bond, Woodward
Bowlew, Reuben
Beene, Jesse
Blackburn, James
Beene, J.P.
Benton, Robinson
Bolding, Marvel
Bloodworth, W.B.
Brason, Joshua

Cockram, M.R.
Clements, Lewellyn
Colston, Samuel
Clarke, E.R.
Calicoat, Claiborne
Carter, John
Carrington, Samuel

Cameron, John
Cock, W.M.
Carrett, Moses
Chisholm, A.C.
Clement, Francis
Clanton, Nathaniel
Cheek, Eli
Cobb, Stansel
Calicoat, G.M.
Collins, Joseph
Canady, Frederick
Cleaveland, S.C.

Douthet, W.W.
Dean, Jefferson
Davis, Nelson
Donrdon, John W.
Donrdon, John, Sr.
Duke, William R.
Denton, Smith
Darby, I.D.
Doaks, J.M.
Devers, George
Dunn, James
Dean, Bedford
Derrick, John

Ellison, Samuel
Edwards, Nathaniel
Edenton, Robert
Edwards, Isaiah
Edwards, William
Edwards, N.W.

Foot, Shobell
Forasure, Charles
Foster, Edwin
Fly, William
Frasure, Dickinson
Ferguson, James
Flack, S.
Forbes, James
Ford, P.H.
Floyd, William

Gates, Isaiah
Goff, Ira

Gray, W.B.
Garth, Jesse B.
Gray, I.M.
Godfrey, Richard
Gentry, Johnson
Guess, Martin
Galaspy, Samuel
Gates, Samuel
Galloway, Moses

Humphreys, William
Hanks, Hansford
Humphreys, George
Houland, Thomas
Helms, Jonathan
Haile, L.
Horn, Jeremiah
Haile, Shadrick
Harland, Ellis
Hermon, A.R.
Harrison, Sterling
Hanks, George
Hamilton, William
Henderson, James
Henderson, Murray
Hasting, Green
Hutson, James
Hutson, Peter
Hearne, William
Harrison, Reuben
Hatson, Howell
Harris, Thomas
Harris, John
Harris, Amos
Huckerby, Green
Harlen, Jacob
Hendrick, Linsey
Hewel, George W.
Hewel, John
Hismith, Elias
Hartgraves, Steven
Hollan, Asa
Hortense, P.H.
Hartgroves, Hugh
Hansborn, D.C.

Ingram, N.B.

Jones, Burrell
Johnson, David
Johnson, John
Jones, A.K.
Johnson, Grif
Johnson, Pleasant
Johnson, Larkin

Kirkman, Snitha
Kirkindal, Jacob
Key, T.M.
Kirkpatrick, John

Lacy, Thomas
Logan, Flemin
Lockridge, Andrew
Lovelady, Thomas
Lacy, Robert
Logan, Posy
Legatt, William
Lackard, William
Lake, H.S.
Laughten, Dudley
Laughten, William
Loggin, Henry
Logan, Joseph
Logan, Aaron

Minter, Ebenezer
Murnell, Benjamin
Morrow, William
Micky, Allen
May, Robert M.
McCaslin, Alfred
McKennell, B.R.
McMinn, Robert
Metcalf, William
McMacklin, T.C.
Mitchell, William
McGee, Samuel
Moore, M.D.
Mathews, Jacob
Maxwell, William
Malone, R.C.
Mabry, David
Mabry, John K.
Martin, M.D.
McCreeder, Carles
Mitchell, Sarah
Moody, Joshua
McLemore, H.C.
Minter, William
McRackin, Robert
Moore, W.T.
Martin, Rebecca
Mabry, John K.
Morgan, Thompson
Morgan, George
Miller, James L.

Nichols, Richard

Nichols, Richard
Norman, William
Nessbitt, A.B.
Nelson, G.C.
Neeley, Cicero
Nation, Joseph
Nation, Balas
Newson, Ranson
Newson, Caswell

Osburn, Zachariah
Odames, Jacob
Obannon, John
Osborn, Nathaniel

Parker, Alexander
Parker, Leonard
Parkerson, James
Peel, James
Person, Henry
Perryman, John F.
Pardin, John
Perry, Susan
Person, John
Perry, Moses
Powers, L.B.
Powers, Thomas
Powers, Nianears
Patton, James K.
Pittman, William
Pittman, Ephiram
Potter, Absalom
Pate, Richard

Reynolds, Simon,
Reed, John
Richy, Robert
Robeson, Orhabel
Rayburn, D.M.
Ray, Mardoc
Renshaw, Richard
Rhea, Hiram
Robinson, John
Rowsy, John
Read, William
Ragsdale, L.B.
Rosy, Ezekiel
Robinson, Ezekiel
Read, George
Read, John
Rafity, Robert
Runnells, H.D.
Reynolds, Simeon

Read, John
Richy, Robert

Skinner, Josiah
Sims, James
Sorrells, David
Smith, Stephen
Sorrells, William
Simons, Henry
Shary, Alexander
Smith, John
Stone, William
Stafford, Joel
Sanders, Drewry
Scott, James
Smith, H.C.
Swaringen, Samuel
Swaringen, William
Swaringen, John
Scott, Thomas S.
Stewart, Charles S.
Sartheres, William
Smithers, Lewis.

Truett, William
Sep. Therlkield
L.B. Tucker
Talbert, Hilliary
Babb, Sandy
Tabb, John
Tucker Thomas I.
Taylor, Sam
Taylor, Henry
Trotter, James
Turnbull, Judah
Turnbull, Jesse
Terry, Willis
Terry, John
Terry, J.M.
Thompson, Josep
Trout, Christopher
Tyler, ----
Trout, Adam

Vaughn, Thomas
Vaughn, John

Williams, W.R.
Woods, N.B.
Weaver, Josiah
Willis, John
Williams, John L.
Walker, Allen
Woods, John B.

Williams, Robert
Williams, Mark
Williams, David
Williams, John
Williams, M.P.
Williams, John L.
Williams, Y.W.
Williams, Henry K.
Wilkins, James
Webster, William M.
Walkup, John
Wheeler, John

Warner, David
Warner, J.T.
Wyatt, William S.
Wood, John B.
Walker, Allen
Woody, Moses

York, Jonathan
York, Y. (?) W.

(Upton, John)

(Tax list for Yalobusha County, Miss., 1834-1835.)

Andrew Hare, of Kentucky, was in his lifetime possessed
by virtue of a Spanish title a tract of land in Wilkinson County (then Miss. Territory) of about 800 acres.
Andrew Hare died in 1800, leaving one child, John Hare,
and his widow Margaret, the mother of John, formerly Margaret Bryant, and sister to Phoebe Hunter, Thomas Bryant,
Moses Bryant, Benjamin Bryant and Mary Bryant.
Andrew Hare is reported to have left a will, which was de-
stroyed by fire in Lexington, Kentucky, but a copy was pre-
served and proven by as exhibited by Gen. Bodley, a witness
since deceased. The bill states that Margaret Hare, the widow, died in year 1801 or 1302, her son, John Hare, died in
1806, eleven years of age, and that his mother's brothers
and sisters are heirs at law.

The legislature of Georgia, in 1784, passed an act by which
William Downs and others were appointed commissioners to
examine the country in Tennessee Bend, issue warrants and
make surveys. These services were performed, and in 1785
an act was passed by the same legislature, allotting each
of these commissioners 10,000 acres of land for their services, to be located by them on Tennessee River. Before
the locations were made, this tract of country was ceded
by Georgia to the general government, in consequence of
which the commissioners could not make location or perfect
their titles. William Downs sold his claim to his sons
Joseph and Henry, and Joseph transferred to Henry. In
1824 Congress recognized the claims of William Downs, who
had previously departed this life, and authorized his heirs
and legal representative to enter in any office of Alabama
or Mississippi, 5000 acres of land.

Claiborne County. ---Martin claimed a final certificate
from the United States, in favor of one Pipes, and it was
admitted that Martin was the legal assignee of said certificate. It appeared from the patent that on 14 August,
1794, Baron Carondelet, acting governor of Louisiana and
West Florida, granted to John Savage, 1000 arpens of
land, situate in the district of Natchez--- bounded east
by land of Patrick Logan, and on the other sides by land
belonging to the crown. The claim was surveyed by the Spanish surveyor, Trudeau. Survey was made March 1, 1794.
A certificate of confirmation by the board of commissioners
was also read. It was dated June 25, 1805, and said confirmation was made to Richard King, as purchaser of Savage.

Jefferson County, 8 March, 1836. William Scott, admr.
of Eliza Lucretia Calvit, filed a bill in court against
Sarah Calvit, James G. Wood and Daniel Hunt. He states
that in 1821, Thomas Calvit, under whom complainants'
intestate claims title to estate sued for, made his last
will and testament in which he made certain bequests
but left the greater portion of his estate undisposed.
Wood and Hunt, who never qualified, were named as exocu-
tors. That a certain Samuel Calvit and Eliza Lee Calvit
were the only heirs at law. The said Samuel Calvit died
in 1826, having had possession of the estate of his father
from time of his death. He made a will in which his wife,
Sarah Calvit, one of the defendants, was made executrix.
Said Sarah took possession of the whole estate of said
Samuel, including that of Thomas Calvit. Eliza Calvit during this time was an infant, and was such at the time of
her death in 1833.

Warren County. The appellees filed their petition in probate Court of Warren County, on the 26th of March, 1838,
praying assignment of dower in certain land and tenements.
They state that Sylvia C., one of the petitioners, was a
widow of Hartwell Vick, dec'd., who was seised and possessed of lands described, during coventure with Sylvia C.,
and that since his decease, she has married William Doss,
appellee. Hartwell Vick received land by purchase from
heirs of Newit Vick.

In year 1810, Thomas L. Norris died, leaving a widow, Ann
Norris, several children and an estate considerably em-
barrassed. The widow married -----Fogle. In 1812 she turn-
ed over management of estate to her brother-in-law, James
Norris, who improved the condition and made final settlement in 1818. After death of Fogle, widow married---Lisson,
and soon afterwards died. Samuel Robb became her administrator. Jefferson County(?)

Amite County. William King was administrator of the estate
of Joseph King, and gave Henry Cassells and Agrippa Gaydon
as sureties. In 1817, Orphans Court affected to annul first
bond and directed a new one which was executed with David
Lea and Richard Hurst as sureties. In 1819 William King
died , and by his will appointed John Lurton, Executor,
who qualified and gave John Lowry and William Stewart, as
sureties..

A marriage contract was entered into by Timothy Kimball
and Margaret Ragan- that property of said Margaret to be
disposed of as she saw proper. This was signed 18 Sept.
1828. In year 1834, Margaret Kimball institutes suit
against her husband to recover certain slaves. During

progress of the suit Margaret Kimball dies and Alfred
King is named as administrator of her estate.

Adams County. John P. McNeil bequeaths to his brother
3/8 of his estate. To his natural son, John Rutherford
McNeil, he gives $10,000. The brother lived in Christian
County, Kentucky. Suit was tried in 1834.

J.J. Cable vs Martin and Bell.
Heirs of Jacob Cable, their father, who died in 1809, leav-
complainants and their mother surviving. Widow and Jesse
Cook were administrtors; Cook died in 1810. The widow married David H. Bell, who took over estate. Mrs. Bell died
about a year later.

In the year 1805, William Brocus, Sr., then a citizen of
Claiborne County, made and executed a will in which he
states:" I give and bequeath to my only daughter Ann,
so long as she may live, for the support of herself and
children, the plantation cn which I now live, with negroes,
Pitcher, Sambo, Charlotte, Mary, Fortune, Phil and Cine,
and when it may please the Almighty when her dissolution
may take place, I desire that the before mentioned seven
negroes and their increase shall revert to gross estate
and be disposed of as hereafter set forth. After death of
daughter Ann I bequeath to my beloved grandsons, Stephen
and William Minor.
(Stephen Minor died in year of 1821 and Ann, his mother,
died in 1831.)

Claiborne County -- Magruder and Nichols vs Stewart, Admr.
Suit to recover slaves under will of William Brocus, Sr.
In will of William Brocus, Sr., bequest of certain negroes
to daughter Ann. Testimony proved that daughter Ann died
in 1831. It further appeared that Ann, dau. of William
Brocus, Sr., had married several times--- to Brashear, by
whom she had one child, a daughter, who married Arthur Car-
ney; they had one child, a daughter Elizabeth, who married
Joseph Nichols, one of the plaintiffs, and is still living.
Ann, dau. of William Brocus, Sr., next marriage was to----
Harrington, by whom she had one daughter, who married Thomas
B. Magruder, the other plaintiff, and is also living.
The last marriage of Ann (dau. of William Brocus, Sr.) was
to ----Tabor, no issue.

Sarah Armfield (formerly Sarah Gustavus)married Isaac
Armfield, March 24, 1825.(Prob. Copiah County)

1830. Resin Hood purchased a tract of land in Yazoo

County of Nancy Bowman and minor children, widow and heirs of Richardson Bowman. No dates.

Elizabeth Pulliam, by next friend, Joseph Leroy, complains that on March 6, 1836, she married Albert B. Pulliam, who was destitute of property. At the time of marriage Elizabeth was entitled as one of the heirs of her father, John Robb, late of Louisiana, also one of the heirs of her mother, Hannah Robb, who died 12 Dec. 1836.

Lyman Harding, former husband of Elizabeth Harding, died leaving a large estate, real and personal, the said wife and only son, Winthrop Harding, were the only legatees. In 1828 the widow married Daniel Vertner, and in 1828 or 1829, paid to Winthrop Harding the whole claim to his father's estate.

Franklin County. --Orphans Court--   -- Gibson was granted letters of administration on estate of Cornelius Spring. At the hearing Ann Byrd, sister of Cornelius Spring, renounced her rights to administer in favor of her son, William Byrd. ---- Gibson was a brother of Mrs. Spring, the wife and former administratrix of Cornelius Spring.

Jefferson County.   Rush Nutt made a will that was probated in Jefferson County, by a mistake there were but 2 witnesses, the testator and Dr. Savage, who drew the will. By will Haller Nutt is sole devisee and legatee. Mary Nutt, the widow, by a marriage contract was to have 1/7 part of estate. At the time of the decease of testator, his heirs, independent of the will were- Mary A. Mason, Sara, Eliza and Margaret Nutt, to each daughter he bequeathed $10,000, besides education and maintenance. Emma Nutt half sister of the other children of Rush Nutt), who died an infant, leaving her half brothers and sisters her heirs. Rittenhouse Nutt (son of Rush Nutt), no provision is made, having received his portion during life time of testator.

Claiborne County. March, 1819.   Elijah Bland made a contract with James A. Maxwell, for 3 lots in the town of Port Gibson, known as Blands Tavern. Bland died and widow Elizabeth and Benjamin Smith took out letters of the administration of the estate. Widow Elizabeth Bland later married John Coursey.

October 2, 1829. Nelson Gillespie filed a bill of complaint, in court of Western district at Natchez, against John B. and George W.Nevitt. It is alleged that the complainant on the 10th day of May, 1829, purchased in fee of John Minor, executor of Katherine Minor, executrix of the last will and testament of Stephen Minor, decd., about 87 acres of land near the city of Natchez, on the Mississippi River, which land was granted by the government of Spain, in the year 1794, to Manuel de Leinas, and under which grant Stephen Minor claimed title by transfer to him about the year 1800, and which grant was subsequently confirmed by commissioners under the authority of the United States.

Warren County. Minerva Wren, admx. of Bellfield Wren, decd., at the time of his death, declared in the circuit court of Warren County, in debt against Charles Span and Susan Span, admrs. of Robert Span, decd., at the time of his death, upon a writing obligatory made by said Robert Span on August 31, 1822, to said Bellfield Wren, then living, by which he promised to pay said Wren a certain sum. In Feb., 1827, letters of administration were granted to defts. on estate of their intestate, Robert M. Span, and on Feb. 28, 1827, defts. published in newspaper of Vicksburg, State of Mississippi., a notice requiring all persons having claims against the estate to exhibit the same.

Wilkinson County, 1830. Jacob R. Holmes, survivor of the late firm of J. Remson, Holmes & Jeremiah Hunt, vs Asher P. Slocum, admr. of Charles Slocum, decd. The plft. declared upon a note executed to Holmes & Co., by decedent and Joseph Wren (not served in the action), dated May 1, 1819.

There was a suit at law in favor of Hezekiah Harrington as executor vs Jeptha Harrington for the recovery of certain slaves, part of the estate. Jepthah Harrington, in his own rights and as administrator, and John Harrington instituted a suit in chancery against Hezekiah Harrington and other legatees under the will, and to establish a prior gift of said estate by deed. From deed: Sarah Bradford, on the 19th of Jan., 1823, made following deed, towit: Sarah Bradford, formerly Sarah B. Coob, of the State of Mississippi, county of Amite, for and in consideration of the good will and affection I have and do bear my nephew, Jephthah Harrington, of said county and state, do give unto said Jephthah Harrington 7 negroes. I give unto Gabriel Harrington, of same county and state, 4 negroes. Unto young John Harrington, a negro woman with all her issue and with all my household goods and chattells in my dwelling house.

It appeared from the bill, answers and exhibits,
that in the year 1819, Newit Vick, being the owner of
two tracts of land in Warren County, lying on the
Mississippi river, proceeded to lay off a town on what
is now Vicksburg.

Newit Vick died in 1819 and by his will directed that
200 acres on the upper part of the uppermost of said
river tracts to be laid off into town lots by his Ex-
exutors to pay his debts and other engagements, in pref-
erence to other properties. He appointed his wife, Elizabeth Vick, son Hartwell and nephew Willis Vick, his executors. Elizabeth Vick died a short time after her husband and Hartwell Vick appeared in orphans court of the
county of Warren, October, 1819, and refused to take upon
himself executorship and renounced the same. Letters test-
amenentary were granted Willis Vick.

In 1821, Willis Vick petitioned the court to be discharged from his executorship, which was refused by the court,
from which decision John Lane, one of the distributees in
right of wife, daughter of testator, appealed to Supreme
Court of Warren County, which court discharged Willis Vick
from executorship, and granted John Lane letters of administration.

Newit Vick left 13 children- 9 daughters and 4 sons,
a dau. who married John Henderson, dau. married Henry Moore,
dau. Mary Vick, unmarried, dau. married John Lane.
Son William Vick became of age in year 1828, son Newit
Vick, still a minor, son Hartwell, son Wesley and son
William, who became of age in 1828. (Wesley became of age
in 1827).

December, 1843. Administration of estate of Jesse Brown,
dec'd. Mention is made of land in Yazoo County.
Admr: Nancy Brown, Fisher Beverly, R. Grayson.

December, 1843. David Stacy appointed admr. of estate of
Charles Lee, who died in 1836, in Miss. leaving a large
estate in Louisana and Mississippi. Ann Lee widow of Chas.
Lee.

Sarah Blanton died seised of about 500 acres of land in
the county of Jefferson, died intestate in said county
in the year 1826. William Blanton was appoined by Orphans
Court of Jefferson County, as administrator.

F.A. Browder and Harriet Hooks, married Sept. 1826. She
died in year 1830. He became admr. of her estate until
his death, February, 1831.

Wit: Robert Liles, Susan Liles, Azella Martin." Deed recorded in Amite County.

Wilkinson County. Heirs of Lewis Davis vs Patrick Foley.
Robert Davis, Lewis Davis, Susannah Guartly, Martha Mc-
Clausland, are heirs of Lewis Davis, dec'd. The complain-
ant states that Lewis Davis, dec'd., did make a will 3
Feb., 1784, possessed of considerable estate, all of which
Martha Davis, widow of testator, continued in possession
until 1790, at which time she married Patrick Foley.
June Term of Court, 1818.

Warren County. Ann Hicks, Admrtrx. of P.C. Hicks, vs
Murphy for Moore. December Court, 1818.

Martin Hackler, dec'd., former husband of the wife of Lewis Cabel, settled on land in question, now county of Jefferson, in the year of 1797. After death of Martin Hackler,
his widow, the present Mrs. Cabel, was natural guardian of
Charlotte May, Samuel, Anna, Maria, Jacob and Esther Hackler, heirs of Martin Hackler. dec'd. Court, 1821.

Claiborne County. Moses Lee and Joseph Montgomery were
partners in 1804. Moses Lee died Feb., 1807. C.S. Lee,
admr. of estate of Moses Lee, filed suit vs Joseph Montgomery in Claiborne County, 1822.

December, 1822. Note of Huldah S. Covington, now wife
of Thomas Calvit in 1820.

Adams County, December Court, 1822. George Winn vs Cole
Heirs. James Cole petitioned for land, June 5, 1795,
from Spanish government, executed by survey, Oct. 3,
1795. Suit by descendants for land.

Wilkinson County, Oct. 18, 1813. In the year of 1791,
Robert Stark obtained from the Governor General of the
province of Louisiana a warrant for 2000 acres of land,
then Natchez District, now Wilkinson County, William
Dunbar, surveyor. Descendants of Robert Stark brought
suit to prove title to land.

Sam'ol Cabin by deed of gift conveyed seven negroes to
Peter Chambliss, Sr., in trust for Peter Chambliss, Jr.,
John Chambliss and Elizabeth Chambliss, children of
Peter Chambliss, Sr., and nephew and niece of said Samuel
Cabin. John Shanks married Elizabeth Chambliss, who
died before attaining her eighteenth birthday.

1831 Court. Louisa Holmes states that she married William Holmes in May, 1826.

Claiborne County Court, 1839. It appears from patent that on August 14, 1794, Govenor of Louisiana and West Florida granted to John Savage 1000 arpens of land in Natchez district, a certificate of confirmation under commission appointed by Congress. In June 25, 1805, said confirmation to Richard King as purchaser of Savage.

Heirs of Charles Land vs Heirs of Thomas Land.
This bill is filed by heirs of Charles Land and charges that their ancestor purchased from Betsy Beames, or Istanchi, her reservation, under treaty of Dancing Rabbit Creek. Heir of Charles Land was Johnson Cyrus Land.

Indenture made Nov. 10, 1836, between Benjamin Williams, of the county of Madison and State of Mississippi, of the first part, Jane Hoggatt, of County of Adams, the second part, F.L. Claiborne, of Adams County, the third part.
A marriage is intended to be solemnized between the said Benjamin Williams and Jane Hoggatt ------ it is there intention to assign and secure to the separate use and disposition of said Jane Hoggatt all and every portion of her real and personal property.

William M. Mercer, admr. of estate of B. Farran, dec'd. vs Theodore Stark. Deposition of Carter Beverly in Feb.1829, wherein he stated that B. Ferran (Farran) was his son-in-law. Suit was started in 1841.

Philip Torrey vs Ann Minor -1842.
Stephen Minor,of Claiborne County, owned a tract of land on which he resided previous to 1814, and that previous to that time he married Ann Gibson, daughter of Samuel Gibson.

Edward Shaw and wife, administrators, vs Simeon Thompson. Edward Shaw and wife Mahala, late Mahala Powell, state in their bill (Holmes County, 1834) that letters of administration was granted to widow of --- Powell, that afterwards she married Shaw. Martha Ann and Samuel Powell were infants.

Franklin County, 1830-1834. William Whitehead and wife, formerly Emily Cade, admrtrx. of estate of Stephen Cade, decd. vs John Cade and John Baker.

Adams County, Jan. 15, 1831. Ellen Miles, admrtrx. of David Miles, dec'd., brought suit against Hugh Jones, admr. of Thomas Jones, dec'd.

Circuit Court, Wilkinson County. Lewis Cason, admr. of Samuel Wright, dec'd., vs Alfred T. Moore and wife Mary. Samuel Wright had been guardian of defendants wife, at that time Mary Singleton, daughter of R. Singleton. Letters of guardianship were revoked in 1827. Date of suit 1834.

Wilkinson County, 30 April, 1830. Judgment in favor of Lemuel Pitcher, admr. of estate of James Dixon, dec'd vs James Shaffer and wife Lucy, admrs. of Robert Spurlock, decd.

William B. Minor and wife Elizabeth, executors of Benjamin Bullen, decd., on April 5, 1828, commenced an action in circuit court of Adams County vs Joseph E. Davis.

Wilkinson County. Caleb Howell, for use of William Stumps, vs H. Eggleston, admr. of Horatio Gildart, decd. For a collection of a note given to Caleb Howell by Horatio Gildart, Feb. 18, 1823.

Adams County Court, 1833. Margaret Biggs vs James Berthe on a note given 12 April, 1829, in Jefferson County, for the use of the estate of Armstrong Ellis, decd.

John Brooks and William Brooks (minors) by their next friend, Winston Gilmore; vs Samuel W. Lewis. Bill of complaint states that in the year of 1822, Nazra Pool and Bluford Brooks became administrators of the goods and chattels of William Brooks, father of complainants. That in February, 1824, the guardian of the complainant, Nazra Pool, had married their mother, and who had obtained an order for division of property among didtributees, had removed with his wards to Louisiana, where they remained until 1830, when they returned to Wilkinson County.

Caroline Mellons, admtrx. of J. Caldwell vs J.P.Gilbert and Eliza Breckinredge, admrs. of Meredith Breckinredge. Hinds County, 1833.

Copia County. Suit brought by Marshall to recover a slave from Fulgham. Plaintiff claimed under a deed of gift from Jesse Fulgham to plaintiffs wife, dated Jan. 17, 1824, recorded in office of register of deeds in Henry County, Ala.

Jesse Fulgham (uncle to deft.) and under whom the plft.
also claimed as donee, which deed was dated Oct. 4, 1804,
and reserved to the donor and his wife Mary, a joint life
interest in property conveyed.

The appellant filed his bill in the court below to recover
a tract of land in Adams County, as the heir of one Mark
Iller, decd. The bill states that Mark Iller, decd., who
is represented to be the ancestor of the complainant, died
in the year 1798. That he obtained possession of the land
in controversy under a title derived from the Spanish government. While the complainant was a minor, one Jonas Iller,
since deceased, pretended to be legal represenative of Mark
Iller, sold land to Job and Jeremiah Routh. Several witnesses testified to marriage of Mark Iller to Mrs. Hootsell, who
was admitted to be the mother of appellant. The marriage
ceremony was performed at the military post of Arkansas, by
a person who testified that he was authorized at this place
to solemized marriages. Birth of appellant (Abraham Iller)
also proved- born between the years 1780-1785. Wit: Christopher Miller, Susanna Smith, J. Bradley, Margaret Williams,
Margaret Bolton-afterwards Margaret Milburn.

Peter Pressler after making will died, leaving wife Elizabeth and daughter Jaily Ann, surviving him. "All estate
to be kept together in the hands of my Executors until
daughter Jaily Ann becomes of lawful age or marries, then
property to be divided between loving wife Elizabeth,
should daughter die without issue then wife Elizabeth to
enjoy property. Exrs: wife, James Buford." Buford qualified but wife renounced. Pressler died in 1824 and in
1826, widow Elizabeth married Robert James, who took and
kept possession of the property until his death, and the
appellees, Narcissa James and Margaret James, are the only
issue of that marriage. Robert James died in 1831, and in
1832 his widow married appellant Scott, and died Oct., 1834,
leaving Scott surviving. In 1832, after marriage of mother
with Scott, Jaily Ann Pressler died at age of fifteen years.
The appellees filed their bill for the purpose of recovering
a portion of property left by Pressler to their mother.

A certain John Vick died without children or descendants
of them, made a will whereby he emancipated certain slaves
and with other not emancipated. John W. Vick was appointed
executor. From will- "All estate not disposed of to be
given brother Burwell Vick, under control and management
of said John W. Vick." Suit filed 4 Dec. 1837.

Claiborne County- A certain tract of land sold by the
United States to Simeon Newman, under whom Sally Newman claims title. Gibson Foster, the ancestor of the ap-

pellees, who claim an undisputed title to fractional
section in same township.

Adams County. Ownership of slaves.
In will of Mrs. Margaret McConell, in which she devised a
tract of land and bequeathed several negroes to her 2
grandchildren, William C. McConnell and Margaret Caroline
Allen, wife of Oliver H. Allen, with provision that if
either died without issue, the property should belong to
survivor. Grandson William McConnell died without issue
before death of Mrs. Allen.

Wife of Thomas Wooldridge claims dower in certain lands
purchased by Thomas Wooldridge from John J. Wilkins and
Gibson C. Wooldridge (bro. of Thomas) on 28 Dec. 1829.
Thomas Wooldridge was appointed consul to one of the ports
in Texas and removed there in 1835, and died in 1836.

John Edgerill and Arthur Carney had been partners in mercantile business. Edgerill began suit in year 1802, in
Mississippi Territory, against Carney for an accounting
of partnership. In 1803 before any decree or payment was
made, Carney died and wife administered estate, she afterwards married John Cummins, who acted as admr. in right
of wife until 1812. Edgergill died in 1807, and suit re-
newed in the name of Prosper and Richard King. The Kings
obtained a degree against Cummins and wife, Joseph Nichols
and his wife, who was a daughter of Carney.

Lydia Whitehead, widow of William Whitehead, filed her petition in probate court, of Franklin County, claiming real
and personal property belonging to the estate of William
Whitehead, decd. Whitehead had been married twice, and
there were several children by first wife, none by the
second. Administrators of Whitehead filed an answer setting
up a marriage contract as a bar to claims of dower.
Marriage contract was made by William Whitehead and Lydia
Whitehead, then Lydia Cade, of Franklin County, 24 Aug.1832.

In Nov., 1835, James C. Dickson died leaving a large estate
in stock, farming utensils and 56 slaves. His only children were, Michael, David and Martha Ann Dickson. Feb. 23,
1836, Jacob Womack obtained letters of administration and
guardianship of said estate. Shortly afterwards Martha
Ann Dickdon married Joseph W. Miller. In summer of 1836,
Jacob Womack died intestate, and Martha Womack (his widow),
and Abraham Womack, Sr. administered on his estate.
L.L. Taylor married widow of Jacob Womack.

Valentine C. Ray died the latter part of 1836, leaving will and testament, duly proven in the county of
Warren. All real and personal property to wife, Martha,
who later married James Simmons.

Charles A. Weston died in 1837, in Yazoo County, leaving
large estate. He had been engaged in the mercantile business in county of Holmes. Letters of administration
granted to ---Hamer and---Blue.

August 26, 1834. Isaac Ross made a will ` which he at-
tached several codicils. Legatees: Adelaide Wade (gr.
daughter), to have $10,000, slaves and negro woman,
Gracie and all her children, living at the time of my decease, unless said negro woman Gracie should elect to go
to Africa, as hereafter provided; Hannibal (negro man)
and his three sisters to be cared for and maintained during their lives by my granddaughter, Adelaide Wade; Enoch
(slave) to be free and to be given $500; provision made
for other slaves to go to Africa under direction of American Colonization Society. In codicil mention is made of
grandson, Isaac Ross Wade. Exrs: Daniel Vertner, James
P. Parker, Dr. Elias Ogden, Isaac Ross Wade, John Coleman.
Wit: John B. Coleman and Peter C. Chambliss.
Codicil. My daughter Margaret A. Reed to have use and
occupation of house wherein I now reside, with all offi-
ces, buildings appertaining to it. March 16, 1835.
Isaac Ross died Jan. 19, 1836, leaving 3 heirs- Jane B.
Ross, Isaac A. Ross and Margaret Reed. Margaret Reed died
before commencement of suit, leaving her interest in estate
to Butler and Duncan. Margaret Reeds will was probated
June 14, 1838. (Jefferson County).

A.B.J. Alston died in the state of Tennessee, leaving
widow and two infants. By his last will and testament
he appointed his brother, J.J. Alston, guardian of children. The widow married C.A.Foster and removed to Mississippi. Foster and wife went to Tennessee and with arm-
ed force and took the children, Mary H. and Ann S.J.
Alston to Holly Springs, Mississippi.

William Barrows, of Madison County, died intestate, leaving widow and heirs at law. Widow was Lydia A. Barrows,
who intrusted estate to her son, Samuel Barrows, who left
for Texas in 1838.

Adams County.

Barger, John	Private. Tenn. Militia. Transferred from West Tennessee
Andrews, John.	Private. 6th U.S. Infantry.
Forrester, Charles	Private. 2nd U.S. Infantry.
Freame, Thomas	Sergt. Rev. Army. First placed on pension March 4, 1795.
Freame, Thomas	Sergt. Rev. Army. Placed on pension April 24, 1816.
Morris, Henry, Jr.	Rev. Army. First U.S. Rifles
Smith, Ebenezer	Rev. Army. First U.S. Rifles.
Burns, James	Private. Pennsylvania Cont'l.
Colter, John	Private. Pennsylvania Cont'l. Died March 26, 1831.
Goodwin, Benjamin	Sergt. Virginia.
Hawley, Samuel	Private. Mass. Transferred from Ind.

Amite County.

Lowry, Robert J.	1st Lieutenant. Miss. Dragoons. Died Dec. 20, 1825.
Wittington, Jarratt	Private. South Carolina. Died Dec. 15, 1831
Morehouse, Jacob	Private. New Jersey. D. June 13, 1832.
Splune, Thomas	Private. Virginia Cont'l.

Claiborne County.

Bruin, Peter	Major. Va. Cont'l. Died Jan.27, 1827
Pope, William	Sergt. North Carolina Cont'l.
Fade, John	Private. Pennsylvania Cont'l.
Durosette, Samuel	Dragoon. Maryland Cont'l.
Twiner, John	Private. Maryland Cont'l.

Copiah County.

McClenden, Shadrack	Private. South Carolina Cont'l.

Green County.

Blankenship, Wommock	Private. Virginia Cont'l. Died, Feb. 24, 1831

Jefferson County.

Clower, William   Private. North Carolina Cont'l.
Died Sept. 6, 1832
Johnson, Solomon   South Carolina Cont'l.

Lawrence County.

Lewis, Elisha   Private. North Carolina Cont'l.
Died July 26, 1829
McLeod, Robert   Private. Maryland Cont'l.
Died Dec. 28, 1832
Mires, John   Private. North Carolina.
Died Nov. 20, 1826

Monroe County.

Adams, David   Private. North Carolina. Trans'fd. from
West Tennessee.
Kitchen, John   Private. South Carolina
Pryon, Allen   Private. Tenn. Mounted Rifles

Simpson County.

Abbey, Edward   Private. -----Cont'l.

Warren County.

McClelland, David   Private. Pennsylvania Cont'l.
Died March 4, 1824

Washington County.

Hackett, John S.   3rd Lieutenant. 24 U.S. Infantry.

Wilkinson County.

Daniels, Charles   3rd Lt. U.S.Army. Transfd. from Penn.
Daniels, Charles   U.S. Army. Transfd. to and from N.Y.

Revolutionary Soldiers of Mississippi whose names
were placed on pension list in year of 1831, under
Act of Congress, June 7, 1832.

Adams County.

Hall, James   Private. Rhode Island. Placed on
                     pension 1828.

Amite County.

Goodwin, John   Private. North Carolina. Age 74 years.
Garlington, Christo. Private. Virginia Cont'l. 77 years·
Rhodes, Charles   Sergt. North Carolina Cont'l. 80 years·
Swearingen, Thomas   Sergt. of Calvary, South Carolina.
                     Age 73 years·
Sibley, John   Sergt. of Calvary, S. Carolina. Age 76.
Whittington, Richard Lieutenant, S. Carolina. Age 81.
Whittington, Cornelius Private. S.Carolina. Age 84 years.
Whittington, Grief   Private. S. Carolina. Age 73 years.

Claiborne County.

Briscoe, Philip   Private. Maryland Militia· Age 76 years.
Dotson, Esau   Private. N. Carolina. Age 80 years.

Copiah County.

Ballard, Francis   Private.   Virginia Cont'l. Age 73.
House, Samuel   "   S. Carolina. Age 69 years·
Heath, Thomas   "   Connecticut.   " 72   "
Neeley, Jacob   "   N. Carolina.   " 71   "
Parker, Asaph   "   Connecticut.   " 72   "
Strong, Joseph   "   Massachusett. " 73   "

Franklin County.

Goodson, Benjamin   Private. Massachusett Cont'l. Age 81
King, David   Sergt. & Capt. of Calvary, South
                     Carolina Militia. Age 78 .
Hawley, Daniel   Artificer. Virginia Cont'l. Age 72.

Holmes County.

Evans, Zachariah   Private. N. Carolina Cont'l. Age 70.

Lowndes County.

McBee, Silas	Private.	S. Carolina Militia.	Age 69
Murphy, John, Sr.	"	S. Carolina "	" 87.

Madison County.

Barnes, Solomon	Private.	Maryland Cont'l.	Age 71 years.
Johnson, Caleb	Sergt.	S. Carolina Cont'l."	79 "
Wade, Joseph	Private.	N. Carolina "	" 75 "

Monroe County

Brown, William	Private.	N. Carolina Cont'l.	Age 74.
Conley, Neal	Private.	New Jersey Cont'l.	Age 75.
Gideon, Richard	Private.	S. Carolina.	Age 69 years.
Merrill, John	Private.	N. Carolina Militia.	Age 82.
Randolph, Hugh	Private.	S. Carolina Cont'l.	Age 78.

Pike County.

Carter, Isaac	Private.	N. Carolina Cont'l.	Age 70.

Simpson County.

Courtney, James	Private.	Virginia Cont'l.	Age 69 years.
Dardin, John	"	N. Carolina "	" 71 "
Hargrove, Alex.	"	S. Carolina "	" 74 "
Murphy, Richard	"	N. Carolina "	" 71 "
Wooms, John	"	S. Carolina "	" 72 "

INDEX

Aarons, 78, 86, 92, 95
Abbey, 95, 162
Acres, 42
Adams, 10, 31, 32, 38, 40,
    58, 59, 64, 69, 90,
    126, 139, 162
Adir (Adair), 92
Agar, 21
Ale, 93
Alford (Aleford), 90, 93,
    124, 134
Alfred, 110
Alexander, 19, 20, 30, 31
Allen, 23, 31, 37, 39, 47,
    78, 86, 93, 115, 124,
    125, 159
Allison, 47, 94
Allerton, 78
Allnict, 78
Alney, 17
Alston, 1, 39, 72, 78, 79,
    112, 160
Alvis, 94
Ambler, 137, 138
Andreu, 20, 29
Andrews, 1, 9, 41, 57, 125,
    161
Anderson, 7, 10, 31, 45,
    47, 56, 59, 64, 69
    70, 81, 85, 110,
    125, 128, 142
Anglo, 72
Anhur, 96
Angley, 74
Anjo, 31
Annon, 37
Anthony, 39
Anxtive, 44
Apperson, 73
Arbour, 45
Armstrong, 39, 43, 45, 64
    81, 85, 95, 110,
    119
Armstrut, 51
Armfield, 151
Arnold, 64
Archer, 75, 81, 82, 130
Archard, 70
Arinton, 94

Arundell, 71, 91
Arthur, 89, 96
Ash, 33
Aswell, 43, 46
Athey, 75
Aubrey,
Auffman, 60
Austin, 108, 115

Bacon, 51
Badin, 13
Bailey, 114
Bailee, 16, 34, 50
Bainor, 32
Baker, 14, 23, 24, 26, 46,
    51, 61, 68, 74, 95,
    136, 156
Balaner, 39, 108
Baldwin, 25
Ballance, 49, 50
Ballard, 72, 126
Ballous (Ballow), 94, 95
Bandon, 15
Banks, 11, 44, 73, 87
Banker, 46
Bannoser, 43
Barfiels (Barfields), 119
Barger, 161
Barcus, 84
Barnes, 15, 74, 76, 77, 83
    84, 85, 87, 93, 164
Barker, 34
Barkins, 121
Barnard, 31, 46
Barland, 15, 31, 40, 41, 46
    32
Barton, 37, 112, 119, 120
Bartlett, 38
Barr (Barre), 44, 49
Barrows, 160
Bassett, 78, 82
Baskins, 107
Bates, 58, 67, 71
Battle, 111, 124
Batchelor, 62, 65

Omitted Index